RING OF POWER

RING OF POWER

The Abandoned Child, the Authoritarian
Father, and the Disempowered Feminine

*A Jungian Understanding of
Wagner's Ring Cycle*

JEAN SHINODA BOLEN, M.D.

HarperSanFrancisco
A Division of HarperCollins*Publishers*

FIRST EDITION

Library of Congress Cataloging-in-Publication Data
Bolen, Jean Shinoda.
Ring of power: the abandoned child, the authoritarian father, and the disempowered feminine: a Jungian understanding of Wagner's Ring cycle / Jean Shinoda Bolen.—1st ed.
p. cm.
Includes bibliographical references and index.
ISBN 0–06–250086–4 (alk. paper)
1. Wagner, Richard, 1813–1883. Ring des Nibelungen. 2. Opera–Psychological aspects. 3. Archetype (Psychology) 4. Jung, C. G. (Carl Gustav), 1875–1961. 5. Mythology, Germanic—Psychological aspects. 6. Patriarchy—Psychological aspects. 7. Dysfunctional family psychology. I. Title.
ML410.W15B64   1992
782.1—dc20   91–58154
                                                                        CIP
                                                                        MN

---

92 93 94 95 96 (HAD) 10 9 8 7 6 5 4 3 2 1

"A Ring of Power looks after itself, Frodo. It may slip off treacherously, but its keeper never abandons it. At most he plays with the idea of handing it on to someone else's care. . . . But as far as I know Bilbo alone in history has gone beyond playing, and really done it."

"To its wearer, the One Ring gave mastery over every living creature, but since it was devised by an evil power, in the end it inevitably corrupted anyone who attempted to use it."

From J. R. R. Tolkein's *Lord of the Rings*, Part One

FREYA, *goddess of youth and love, whose apples keep the immortals eternally young. Wotan offers her to the giants as payment for building Valhalla, thinking he can avoid paying the price. Freya is a symbol of the qualities that men sacrifice to acquire power and fame.*

CONTENTS

Preface ix

Acknowledgments xv

INTRODUCTION
The Ring Cycle Is About Us 1

CHAPTER I
The Rhinegold: The Quest for Power and Its
Psychological Cost 15

CHAPTER 2
The Valkyrie: The Authoritarian Father and
the Dysfunctional Family 43

CHAPTER 3
Siegfried: The Hero as an Adult Child 87

CHAPTER 4
Twilight of the Gods: Truth Brings an End to the
Cycle of Power 133

CHAPTER 5
Freeing Ourselves from the Ring Cycle 181

CHAPTER 6
Beyond Valhalla: A Postpatriarchal World? 207

Family Tree 221

*Glossary of Characters, Creatures, Objects,
and Places 222*

Symbology of Scenes 227

Selected Readings 231

Discography 235

Index 237

PREFACE

AS A PSYCHIATRIST AND JUNGIAN ANALYST, I TRY TO RECOG-
nize what rings true psychologically. It was with this "ear," and
not that of a musician's with which I heard Richard Wagner's
Ring of the Nibelung. What I experienced was inspired story;
Wagner had created a four-opera dramatic series whose situations, characters, and words were mythic, with the power of
myth to resound in the deepest layers of our psyches. The *Ring*
cycle taps into the emotions of real life and mirrors back to us
themes we live out. I knew that if I could make story and meaning come to life for others, as I had experienced the story and
meaning myself, I could help others have deep insights into
themselves and their significant relationships as well as provide a perspective on the psychological origins and destructiveness of authoritarian institutions. I had in mind a title too long
to actually use but one that does describe what this book is
about: "Ring of Power: The Authoritarian (or Narcissistic)
Father, the Abandoned (or Rejected) Child, the Disempowered
(or Absent) Feminine, and the Dysfunctional Family and
Society."

I also set out to tell the story of the *Ring of the Nibelung*
well. It is a complex and engrossing story that can be compared
to a four-part television miniseries spanning three generations,
or to a Russian novel with many characters and shifts in scenes
and time. While not essential, familiarity with the story before
seeing the opera certainly makes for a deeper, more magnif-
icent experience. Before each opera, I had wanted to read something that would bring the story to life, and I did not find it.

PREFACE

Besides, to accomplish what I wanted to with this book, it was crucial to convey the story to the reader in such a way that the story would evoke feelings, images, and personal memories. To do this, I would be a storyteller. Thus, I begin each of the four central chapters by telling the story of one of the four operas — *The Rhinegold, The Valkyrie, Siegfried,* and *Twilight of the Gods* — that make up the *Ring of the Nibelung.* These are narratives that can be read before seeing the opera, as well as a means of bringing the stories alive before delving into their psychology.

Commentary based upon Jungian archetypal psychology in combination with the psychology of dysfunctional relationships and patriarchy follows the description of each opera in Chapters One through Four. When a connection is made between a story that captivates us and real life, the truth we perceive through it about ourselves, our families, and society can be transformative. Emotional and cognitive insight together then bring the *Ring* cycle home to us with an undeniable force: we now know something to be true.

In opera circles, the *Ring* holds a fascination second to none. The evocative power of music and myth to touch deep chords of personal meaning explains why individuals are enthralled by the *Ring of the Nibelung.* When this is the experience, the soul is moved. When psychological understanding is added, the mind also becomes involved. I have written *Ring of Power* as a means for the psychological realm to enter the conscious awareness of people who want to add this dimension to their experience of the *Ring.*

That the *Ring of the Nibelung* — a work that Richard Wagner devoted four years, from 1848 to 1852, to creating — has throughout its existence been so compelling attests to Wagner's ability to give expression through his music and drama to universal motifs, or archetypal human experiences that are repeated themes in life.

PREFACE

The *Ring* cycle has a devoted, fanatic, loyal following like no other operatic work. Its followers come from all over the world to attend when a complete cycle is scheduled. Perhaps only the Grateful Dead, a famous San Francisco Bay Area rock group, whose fans are known as "Deadheads," has a similar following. When the *Ring* cycle came to San Francisco and people descended upon the opera house, behaving more like fans than staid operagoers, it was perhaps inevitable that they would be referred to as "Ringheads." (Two of the Grateful Dead are themselves "Ringheads.") The excitement generated by the opera was called "Ring Mania," again attesting to the intensity of the fascination with the *Ring of the Nibelung*. During this same period, the Public Broadcasting System was airing a filmed version of the *Ring* cycle given by the Metropolitan Opera, and so for four evenings, the *Ring* was on television as well. Watched, discussed, copied by thousands of VCRs, this series gripped an intelligent television audience in much the same way as "The Power of Myth," Bill Moyer's interviews with Joseph Campbell, had in that series. In both cases, mythic material that had been familiar mainly to scholars, mythologists, Jungians, or Wagnerites became widely accessible to a fascinated public. Viewing audiences were affected by what they saw and heard and then wanted to know more.

The growing receptivity to myth by the general public, along with the growing rejection of managed news as presented to us by our politicians, shows a discernment for truth and depth. Managed news, with its "photo opportunities" and "sound bites," is presented as factual but is really manipulated and often deceptive storytelling. In contrast, myths, with no claim to factuality, tell us the truth the way dreams do—in the language of metaphor and symbol.

My interest in the *Ring of the Nibelung* grows out of the same inspiration that led me to write *Goddesses in Everywoman* and *Gods in Everyman*. In these books, I describe powerful archetypal patterns within men and women based descriptively upon Greek gods and goddesses and show how they interact with patriarchal values that reward some archetypes and punish others. Because I had written these books, I was asked to speak about the gods and goddesses in Wagner's *Ring* cycle as part of a symposium cosponsored by Langley Porter Psychiatric Institute, the department of psychiatry at the University of California, San Francisco, where I am a clinical professor, and the San Francisco Opera Company. When I read the libretto and attended the operas, I found myself encountering familiar archetypes from Greek mythology, but with Germanic names and more human and complex personalities.

What I experienced moved me deeply and made me want to articulate what I sensed and intuited. Without consulting me or my publisher, the *Ring of the Nibelung* took over my creative process like an unplanned pregnancy and put *The Grail and the Goddess,* the book I had been working upon, on a back burner.

Thus *Ring of Power* came into being. I expect that readers will find aspects of their personal lives in the first four chapters. I hope that details will be remembered and emotions tapped when parallels are revealed between real life and the *Ring* cycle. While the substance of the book is in these chapters, the central spiritual message of this book can be found in Chapter Five, "Freeing Ourselves from the Ring Cycle."

Ultimately the psychological becomes spiritual after we free ourselves from having to fulfill expectations that are not true to what matters deeply to us and from addictions or complexes that have us in their grip, and come into a sustained relationship with what C. G. Jung called the archetype of the Self. I think of the "Self" as a generic term for the inner experience of god, goddess, Tao, higher power, spirit. The Self by any name is a source of wisdom, compassion, and meaning; through which we know that we have a place in the universe.

PREFACE

Chapter Six, "Beyond Valhalla: A Postpatriarchal World?" is a visionary speculation upon the possibility of a postpatriarchal era and the contribution each of us makes toward that end by living authentically and speaking the truth.

This book, which insisted that I give it birth, now goes out into the world. I hope that it will touch both the heart and mind, that it will evoke dreams, and empower men and women to act upon what is true for them. May *Ring of Power* make a difference to people who can make a difference wherever they are.

ACKNOWLEDGMENTS

PETER OSTWALD M.D. PERSISTED IN HIS INVITATION TO ME TO be part of a symposium on the *Ring of the Nibelung*. Richard M. Childs, M.D. gave me Robert Donington's *Wagner's Ring and Its Symbols*. Patricia Ellerd Demetrios, Ph.D. accompanied me to the *Ring* cycle, and her perceptions, enthusiasm, and knowledge about codependency and recovery literature and groups contributed immeasurably. *Ring of Power* was an unforseen undertaking. Without the invitation, the introduction, and the dialogue, I know this book would not have been written.

I am exceedingly fortunate in having Clayton Carlson as my publisher and Tom Grady as my editor. Their belief in me and support for my work lets me shift from one writing project to another and back, and allows me to be in an organic creative process. Tom Grady gave me valuable editorial advice and suggested Arthur Rackham's illustrations for the cover and book. Valerie Andrews was a perceptive and helpful editorial consultant.

For the text of Richard Wagner's *Ring of the Nibelung*, I used Andrew Porter's English translations commissioned by the English National Opera, and Stewart Robb's translation. My thinking has been shaped by my training as a psychiatrist and a Jungian analyst, by my patients and analysands, by the women's movement, and relatively recently by Alice Miller, who writes poignantly about child-rearing and narcissistic parenting, and by Anne Wilson Schaef on codependency and addictions within the context of society.

ACKNOWLEDGMENTS

Most of all, I marvel at how much acknowledgment must be given to synchronicity and grace, which I have felt to be invisibly and actively present in the conception, incubation, and birth of this book.

RING OF POWER

The Ring Cycle Is About Us

THERE ARE NO GOOD MARRIAGES OR HAPPY FAMILIES IN classical mythology. Everywhere there is hierarchy. An authoritarian father figure is king of the mountain. The chief god acts out of self-interest, imposing his will and desires on others; looked at psychologically, he is a model of an authoritarian, narcissistic personality. Women—as mortals, as goddesses, as feminine symbols—are with few exceptions oppressed, sacrificed, or humiliated. Rape is the norm, and power rather than love is the ruling principle. Sons and daughters either bask in approval when they are obedient extensions of their father's will or are sacrificed, rejected, abducted, punished, or ignored.

The mythology of a culture, in this case Western civilization, instructs us about the values, patterns, and assumptions on which this culture is based. When we stop to examine our mythological heritage, we may be enlightened or appalled by how much it is a metaphor for what

I

exists in contemporary reality, how much our mythology is about us.

The chief god of the *Ring of the Nibelung* is named Wotan, rather than Zeus; his wife is Fricka, not Hera. Brunnhilde, like Athena, is the chief god's immortal warrior daughter and favorite child. While these characters resemble the Greek deities whose mythology is also based on power, there are significant differences. Love, compassion, and wisdom enter the realm of power in the *Ring*. It is a mythology of the dysfunctional family in transition which demonstrates that the quest for power is a substitute for love.

To become immersed in the *Ring of the Nibelung* as opera, music, or story is to have an experience that can be compared to having a series of powerful dreams. We remember the important parts, and that which is truly significant may remain with us vividly. When the meaning becomes clear, an Aha! occurs that informs us why we were fascinated or stirred up by a particular incident and gain insight into some facet of ourselves or our lives that empowers us, as truth does. With the *Ring of the Nibelung*, the same is true, but we can return again and again to the experience itself, each time perhaps drawn to yet another symbol or part of the story, a story that weaves variations on the themes of love and power, themes that run through and affect the lives of us all.

INTRODUCTION

WHY MYTHS?

Myths and metaphors, like dreams, are powerful tools that draw the listener, dreamer, or reader to a character, symbol, or situation, as if in recognition of something deeply known. Myths bypass the mind's effort to divorce emotion from information. They make an impression, are remembered, and nudge us to find out what they mean, accounting for the avid interest that *Ring* audiences have in the meaning of the story.

If the narrative of the *Ring of the Nibelung* or particular parts of it holds some fascination, it can act like yeast in activating deeper levels of the psyche, raising issues, memories, and feelings into consciousness.

In this book, I begin as a storyteller and follow each story with psychological interpretations, in the same way that interpretation follows the telling of dreams in a Jungian analysis. I "amplify" the *Ring of the Nibelung* as if it were a complex dream. My comments about the story are thus suggestions, potential meanings that draw on my knowledge of people, archetypes, and psychological patterns. The authority who knows when an interpretation is true, however, is the person (equivalent to "the dreamer") who recognizes that this part of the *Ring* is her or his story. When an interpretation rings true, it is a discovery that casts light upon life, bringing consciousness that may in turn help us know who we are and what is truly important to us.

INTRODUCTION

THEMES IN THE
RING OF THE NIBELUNG

Each of the four operas introduces variations on the main theme of power versus love and the effect of the quest for power on individuals and relationships. In *The Rhinegold* (*Das Rheingold*), the opera that serves as a prelude to all that happens, the ring of the Nibelung—which becomes the major symbol through all four operas—is forged by Alberich, who is a dwarf, or Nibelung. It is a ring of power; whoever possesses it can rule the world. Whoever forges the ring must renounce love forever. Psychological insight helps us understand how this comes about and why Alberich, who symbolizes the rejected, abused child and the shadow that can accompany us through life, demanding revenge for our childhood humiliations, will pay this price. Alberich represents a dark side of the personality that underlies the quest for power over others. While Alberich forges the ring, Wotan, who is equivalent to Zeus, contracts to build Valhalla as a monument to his power, manhood, and everlasting fame. Wotan thinks that he can avoid paying the price when payment comes due. He had promised to give the builders Freya, the goddess of love and youth, the very qualities usually sacrificed by ambitious men.

The themes in *The Valkyrie* (*Die Walküre*), the second opera in the series, focus on dysfunctional family dynamics caused by the inequality of power and the loss of love. The marriage of Wotan and Fricka (like that of Zeus and Hera) has deteriorated. They keep up appearances, but there is hostility between them. Wotan is an authoritarian father who expects his children to further his ambition. He ignores their difficulties. His young son, Siegmund, is left to fend for himself, and the abandonment of his daughter Sieglinde ensures that she becomes a victim. Like many men in dysfunctional marriages, who turn to daughters who idolize them, Wotan is in an emotionally incestuous relationship with Brunnhilde, his beloved Valkyrie daughter, until she disobeys him out of her compassion for Siegmund and Sieglinde and becomes the object of his wrath and abuse for doing so. We can also see in Brunnhilde the plight and cost of becoming less the archetype and more human, a situation faced by some daughters of successful fathers. Such women often fare well in careers, but at considerable cost to their feminine nature and their individuality.

Siegfried, the third opera, is the name of "the hero who has no fear," who kills the dragon and is a prototype of an emotionally numbed, successful son of a dysfunctional family. He was raised by Mime, a martyr parental figure, who claims to love Siegfried but does not, seeking instead to gain access to power through him. Siegfried has not been genuinely loved and therefore cannot recognize or value unconditional love when he receives it. Thus he (and men like him) will take from and then forget the woman who genuinely loves him, which is what Siegfried does to Brunnhilde in the fourth opera, *The Twilight of the Gods.*

INTRODUCTION

This last opera is more widely known by its German title, *Götterdämmerung*. It makes us realize how events set in motion by Alberich and Wotan in *The Rhinegold* affect individuals down through the generations. We learn of a cosmology that explains patriarchy and realize that a new era can begin only after the old structure is destroyed and the ring of the Nibelung returned to the Rhine. By now, we know that the story is about us, and we are left to muse upon what must be known and what must be done, to bring an end to the ring of power and its destructive influence in our lives and our world.

PEOPLE LIVE OUT THE RING

As a psychiatrist in an analytic private practice, I see "Wotan's wife and his children" often. I see "Wotan" much less often. Wotan does not spend much time in any psychiatrist's office, as he fears looking weak and equates revealing vulnerability with giving up control. I may see him if he becomes "the Wanderer," the identity Wotan assumes when he seeks wisdom after he experiences loss and limitation and becomes less arrogant and depressed as a result.

"Wotan" is another name for an authoritarian personality, a man whose ambitions and need for control affect his family and workplace. The authoritarian personality requires others to see things his way and to put his wants first. His will is enforced by his anger and power to punish, which results in dysfunctional relationships, families, and organizations. When anyone identifies with Wotan as an archetype, an authoritarian personality results. In his presence or sphere of influence, speaking the truth, taking initiative, and authentic expressions of feeling are stifled. Under these circumstances, people often suffer from depression, become codependents to his narcissism, act in a passive-resistant way, numb their feelings, or have psychosomatic illnesses.

Like Fricka, many a contemporary "Wotan's wife" finds that her marriage has form but no substance. Once Wotan is caught up in his ambition—in obtaining his equivalent of the ring of power—he often is not interested in his wife sexually and does not care to know how she feels or what she is thinking. She and her perceptions about the cost of his quest for status, money, or power are discounted. When she tells him the truth, he treats her like a nag; consequently, in an effort to be heard, she may become shrill and sometimes hysterical. In this case, the man usually grows even more distant.

"Wotan's daughters" may be emotionally abandoned and treated as inconsequential, or they may be called upon to take care of their father's emotional needs and become surrogate wives. When daughters are unvalued or abused by a powerful father, whose love and approval they seek, it affects their confidence and self-esteem. It makes them susceptible to later becoming dominated by someone else, the way Wotan's daughter Sieglinde was dominated by Hunding. With father-daughter incest, the likelihood of later physical abuse is even greater. "Wotan's daughters" who bask in their father's approval commonly become "father's daughters," which was Brunnhilde's family role. As such, they can become their father's confidante, closer to him than he is to their mother. Identified with him and his goals, these daughters become reflections of him at the cost of their own individuality.

Since sons often play a part in furthering the long-range ambitions of a Wotan, "Wotan's sons" usually have different problems. The son who comes to a psychiatrist is often like Siegmund in having an absent father, or one he rarely sees. He may differ significantly from his father in his interests and personality traits, as Wotan's son Siegmund certainly did, and at some point may be rejected by his father for not being up to the role for which he was conceived. Low self-esteem and depression are his problems.

"Wotan's sons" who are like Siegfried, Wotan's grandson and heir, are not likely to see a psychiatrist. They do not perceive themselves as having problems. Like Siegfried, they are unfeeling men, who think strategically and logically about what they encounter in the outer world. They are pragmatic thinkers, which gives them an advantage in scientific, sport, business and military careers. They are men who go after what they want, take from others, and move on. If they are sons, grandsons, or surrogate sons of dynasty builders, they may be groomed for success as heirs of Wotan, only to find that he is unable to relinquish control or power.

INTRODUCTION

SYMBOLS OF COMPASSION AND COURAGE: BRUNNHILDE AND SIEGMUND

In the *Ring* cycle, it is Brunnhilde who brings an end to Wotan's era of power, an ending he anticipates but cannot bring about himself. When Valhalla goes up in flames, it can symbolize the end of a personal or family cycle or, as I suggest in Chapter Six, "Beyond Valhalla," a possible end to patriarchy.

In contemporary family life and commentaries upon society, it is "the daughter" who brings to light abuse of power in relationships. Beginning with the emphasis of the women's movement on telling the truth about one's own experience, and now in the context of twelve-step groups as well, people break the cycle of dysfunction in this way. Truth is the purifying fire that brings down the old order.

Although it is the daughter Brunnhilde who brings about change, it is Siegmund, the son who raised himself and followed his own feelings, whose example of selfless love changes her. In *The Valkyrie*, Siegmund renounces his opportunity to be an immortal hero rather than abandon Sieglinde to further suffering. Siegmund is a man whose feelings are not numbed, who uses his sword to defend vulnerability and freedom of choice. Siegmund is the son who does not survive or thrive in patriarchy, the archetype in men that is sacrificed for success, and a prototype of the courageous hero motivated by compassion, who is both an outcast and a model for the nonpatriarchal man. In Siegmund, we see male strength used to protect and care for others.

INTRODUCTION

Brunnhilde and Siegmund, Wotan's daughter and son, suffer firsthand and are courageous. They are motivated by love rather than power or vengeance. They are archetypal figures who need to come into the psyche, the family, and the culture in order to transform them.

ON WANTING LOVE
AND SETTLING FOR POWER

I am convinced that we enter the world seeking to be loved and that we settle for power when we are not loved. The world we enter is a world of relationship. At birth, we arrive in our innocence and vulnerability as babies, designed to evoke the love and nurturing that we need to survive. After birth, life unfolds in a spiral pattern: we repeatedly enter new worlds of relationships—as children, as adolescents, and as adults, each time wanting to be welcomed into this new world and loved. When we find that we are not loved or are loved only for what we do or what we own, power in some form becomes the substitute, the means by which we seek the acceptance and security that love provides freely. Thus we seek to be noticed or needed, to be indispensable or in control.

When people become obsessed by their quest for power as control, security, or recognition, and when they have power over others, then what they do affects those around them, as we see clearly demonstrated in the *Ring of the Nibelung*. Alexander the Great, Napoleon, Genghis Khan, and Hitler, real people who, like Alberich and Wotan, sought to rule the world, affected millions of people in the attempt. A tyrannical parent or an employer with a narcissistic need to control others has a much smaller sphere of destructive influence but can nonetheless be devastating psychologically to individuals.

The life story of anyone for whom power counts more than love takes place in a family, organization, or nation, that is within the patriarchy, the culture that emphasizes dominance of individuals or classes or nations over other individuals, classes, or nations, of ideological supremacy decided by might, and religions that support the divine right of some men to subjugate others and of mankind to subdue nature. Power is the ruling principle in patriarchy, and where power rather than love rules, freedom and justice also suffer. It is a struggle to stay with love as a principle in a patriarchal culture, yet succumbing to power is destructive to the very relationships we came into the world needing. Each individual must struggle to determine whether love or power will be the ruling principle in the psyche. Which will decide our significant relationships, choice of work, place to live, and ultimately, through our choices, what we become? It is not just Wotan, Brunnhilde, Siegmund, and the characters in the *Ring of the Nibelung*, but each of us, who face the same issue of love versus power.

We come into a power-oriented world seeking to be loved. We need others, who may nurture us or harm us, support our growth or hamper it, make us feel safe and inherently worthy, or fill us with doubts and self-loathing.

INTRODUCTION

We also come into the world with an inherent human capacity to love others and to feel good about ourselves when we do love and love what we do. Authenticity and integrity or inner harmony are related to choices made on the basis of who we are and what we love. Depressions, anxiety, madness, lack of self-esteem, feelings of meaninglessness, violence, and addictions that numb the pain and create more pain come when we do not experience ourselves as having choices, cannot love, are split by warring internal factions, and are afraid and have suppressed what we truly feel or fear acknowledging as true. Healing begins with acknowledging the truth of our condition.

TEMENOS AND TRANSFORMATION

The space where I meet my patients is visibly an office. When trust is established, it becomes a *temenos*, which means "sanctuary" in Greek. I am pledged to keep it a safe place for their confidences and vulnerabilities, a place where they will not be exploited or betrayed, where their many parts can find sanctuary, where they can tell the truth. It is a place where psychological armor and weapons can and must be put down if healing is to take place. A recovery program, twelve-step group, women's circle, or men's group can also be a *temenos* for its members. Ideally, families and significant relationships should be as well.

Temenos meant sacred ground; it was a temple, a place where divinity could enter and be felt, equivalent to the

INTRODUCTION

Christian concept that "where two or more are gathered in my name, there shall I be also." Wherever we encounter the unconditional love we came into the world seeking, we are in a sacred space, a *temenos*. Here grace and revelation in their more everyday garb as love and insight can be found.

In the healing precinct of the god Ascelpius at Epidauros in Greece, there was not only a round *temenos* but also an amphitheatre, where those who came could see performances as part of what was prescribed in order to restore health. All supplicants also sought to have a healing dream.

The *Ring of the Nibelung* can play a similar role in psychological healing, as did those performances in the amphitheatre at Epidauros. These four dramas in operatic form have the power of major dreams, as well. They reveal destructive themes in our lives, which we may be able to change once we grasp the pattern and its cost to us. If a powerful series of dreams or archetypal stories are taken to heart, the transformative effect can be enormous. The message hits home, freeing us from unconscious patterns, leading us to appreciate that our lives have meaning, and reminding us that, with consciousness and choice, we can make changes in our personal world, and the world.

THE RHINEMAIDENS *plead for the return of the Rhinegold. In its original state, this symbolic gold is a source of meaning, joy, and numinosity hidden in the depths. To forge the Rhinegold into an instrument of power that can be used to subjugate others is a corruption of it, which charismatic and demonic leaders do.*

THE RHINEGOLD
(DAS RHEINGOLD)

THE QUEST FOR POWER
AND ITS
PSYCHOLOGICAL COST

CAST OF CHARACTERS

THE RHINEMAIDENS
(Three river nymphs whose task it is to guard the Rhinegold):
Flosshilde, Wellgunde, Woglinde

THE NIBELUNGS
(Dark dwarves who live underground in Nibelhome; they mine gold, work at forges, and are craftsmen)
Alberich: *the dwarf who forges the ring of power from the Rhinegold*
Mime: *Alberich's bullied brother who makes the Tarnhelm*

THE IMMORTALS
(Gods and goddesses)
Wotan: *the chief and most powerful Teutonic god, who rules through agreements and treaties carved on his spear. He has one sighted eye, wears a patch over his other, and carries the spear. Known as Odin in Norse mythology, he is a sky-god equivalent of the Greek god Zeus.*
Fricka: *Wotan's wife, goddess of marriage and fidelity, sister of Freia, Froh, and Donner*
Freia: *the goddess of youth and love, who cultivates the golden apples that the deities must eat to retain their youthful immortality; sister of Fricka, Froh, and Donner. Promised by Wotan to the giants as payment for building Valhalla.*
Loge: *in* The Rhinegold *he is a quick-thinking trickster, a demi-god who travels widely and gathers information; in subsequent operas, he is the god of fire.*
Froh: *god of the fields, protective brother of Freia, who creates the Rainbow Bridge to Valhalla*
Donner: *god of thunder and lightning, which he can evoke with his magic hammer; protective brother of Freia*
Erda: *goddess of wisdom, who resides deep in the earth; an earth mother whose influence preceded Wotan's*

GIANTS
two brothers, the last of their race of master builders, who build Valhalla
Fafner: *the dominant brother, who desires power and resents the gods*
Fasolt: *the innocent brother who expects to be treated fairly*

CHAPTER I

THE RHINEGOLD

The Quest for Power and Its Psychological Cost

The Story

THREE LOVELY RIVER NYMPHS, THE RHINEMAIDENS, CAVORT playfully underwater. They teasingly remind each other that they are the guardians of the Rhinegold. A dwarf, Alberich the Nibelung, comes upon them and watches with increasing delight.

Alberich wants to join the river nymphs, but he is rebuffed. They make fun of his appearance, commenting upon his dark skin and ugly appearance. He persists and tries to catch them. They tease him cruelly. One calls him "dearest of men" and lets him caress her. Telling him sweetly that he is "shaped like a toad," she then laughs in his face and darts away. The river nymphs are beautiful, and Alberich yearns for them, chasing them with increasing desperation, as they elude his grasp while making merry cries.

Finally, almost out of control with hurt and rage, Alberich stands at the bottom of the Rhine and shakes his clenched fist at the Rhinemaidens, who swim tantalizingly above him. At that precise moment, the sun strikes what appears to be a rock formation, and the water glows with a diffuse golden light. The

Rhinemaidens react to this with joy and bathe in the brightness, while Alberich's anger turns to curiosity. He is fascinated by the source of the radiance, and asks the river nymphs what it is. They tell him that it is the Rhinegold.

Alberich acts unimpressed, telling them that it is worthless "if shining on their games is all that it is good for." His deprecating comments provoke them to tell him that a man who forges a ring from the Rhinegold will create a ring of power with which he could rule the world. Because of his amorous pursuit of them, the Rhinemaidens mistakenly think that Alberich cannot do what is required to make the ring. Misjudging him (and the effect of their cruelty on him), they reveal the secret: to forge the ring of power, a man must renounce love forever.

Alberich does not hesitate for a moment. He takes the gold and declares that "in order to forge the ring of revenge, I renounce love and curse it." Darkness immediately descends.

WOTAN AND THE COST OF VALHALLA

Now the scene shifts to the mountains, where Wotan and Fricka are asleep. Wotan is dreaming of Valhalla, a great hall and stronghold that will establish "his manhood, his power, and his fame." Far in the distance, the towers of a fortress castle gleam in the morning sun. Fricka awakens first. She is startled at seeing the castle, and she shakes Wotan awake. Wotan opens his one eye, sees the huge building of his dreams, and feels pleasure and triumph. Fricka, in contrast, is anxious and feels Wotan should be also.

"Heedless one, try to remember the price that has to be paid! The castle is ready; the payment is due. Remember what you pledged!" she tells him.

Through Wotan's wife, Fricka, we learn that he had made an agreement with two giants, Fafner and Fasolt. In exchange for building Valhalla, Wotan promised to give them Fricka's sister

Freya, the goddess of love, youth, and beauty. Freya's garden is the source of the golden apples that the deities eat every day; eating the apples keeps the gods eternally young and immortal. Wotan minimizes the problem, blaming Loge the trickster for getting him into this fix and also trusting him to get him out of it.

Called "Allfather" in Germanic mythology, Wotan is a tall and powerful figure who is missing one eye. He carries a large spear with which he rules. Treaties and agreements that Wotan upholds are carved on its shaft. Loge is a quick-thinking demigod with the gift of persuasive speech, and he is often traveling, his whereabouts unknown until he shows up. In this respect, Loge resembles Hermes, the Greek messenger god. Loge is also the god of fire.

Fricka is angry and anxious about what will happen to Freya. She is critical of Wotan, saying, "Nothing is sacred; you men harden your hearts when you lust for might." He retorts, "Didn't you also want the great hall?" To this she responds, "Only because it might have enticed you to stay at home."

When the giants come to collect their payment, Wotan is evasive. When they remind him that he promised them Freya, he says he was only jesting, that she is "too lovely for dolts such as they."

Though they look alike, Fafner and Fasolt are quite different in personality. Fasolt expects to be treated fairly and is momentarily speechless. Then he reminds Wotan that their agreement was carved in runes upon the shaft of his spear. Fasolt yearns for a woman's beauty and love to grace the giants' simple home, while Fafner is motivated by envious hostility. He wants Freya in order to deprive the gods of the golden apples and looks forward to seeing the gods grow old and weak.

Confronted by the giants demanding that he pay up, Wotan counts upon Loge to come up with something the giants would want more than Freya. When Loge finally appears, however, he denies that he promised a solution; saying he only promised to look into it. Loge reports that he has roamed all over the world and has found that "nothing is of greater worth than love." However, he has heard a tale from the Rhinemaidens about a dwarf named Alberich who values a certain ring more than love.

It is a gold ring with such magic power that its owner can conquer the world. With the ring, Alberich has amassed a hoard of gold in Nibelhome, the underground home of the dwarves. On hearing of this treasure, Fafner takes Fasolt aside and forces him to agree to take this gold as payment for Valhalla. Fafner gives Wotan and Loge a day to get the gold. In the meantime the giants will take Freya as hostage, to be forfeited forever if they do not have the gold by evening. As the giants carry her off, Freya is terrified, and she cries and screams for help.

WOTAN AND LOGE VISIT ALBERICH

As soon as the giants leave with Freya, Wotan and Loge descend underground to seek Alberich. Alberich is now a tyrant who has made all the Nibelungs his slaves. He drives them mercilessly to find and mine gold, to smelt and forge it into shapes for him. He has bullied his brother Mime, who cringes in terror, to make the Tarnhelm, a headpiece crafted of beautifully wrought gold. Using the ring, Alberich has imbued the Tarnhelm with magic. It can transform the wearer into anything he desires to be or take him to any place he wishes to go. With it, Alberich has made himself invisible, the better to intimidate, strike, watch, and terrify others.

When Wotan and Loge come upon Mime, he is huddled on the ground whimpering. A large work crew of Nibelungs come into view, driven by Alberich, who is now visible, lashing at them with a whip. Seeing Mime talking with these strangers, Alberich comes over and strikes him, forcing him to join the others.

The two gods draw a mistrustful and wary Alberich into conversation. He brags that he can transform himself into any-

THE RHINEGOLD

thing with the Tarnhelm. Loge, ever the trickster, doubts Alberich and goads him into a demonstration. Alberich puts on the Tarnhelm, says, "Giant snake, coiling and winding!" and disappears in vapor. In his place appears a huge serpent. Wotan laughs, and Loge pretends to be afraid.

When Alberich reappears, he is smug. Loge confesses that he is wondrously impressed and wonders if he can also grow smaller and become quite tiny. Then he adds, "But maybe that's too hard." Alberich rises to the bait and shows off. He dons the Tarnhelm, says "Creeping toad, gray and crooked," and vanishes. When a toad appears, Wotan and Loge grab and capture it. Loge seizes the Tarnhelm, and Alberich suddenly becomes visible in his own shape. While Alberich tries to escape, Wotan holds him down and Loge ties him up.

THE CURSE ON THE RING

Wotan and Loge return from Nibelhome with Alberich as their prisoner. Wotan demands the hoard of gold as ransom for Alberich's freedom. Alberich readily agrees and thinks he is getting off cheap; since he has the ring, he reasons that he can force the dwarves to get him more gold. At his command, the Nibelungs hurriedly bring the gold and heap it up. After all the gold is on the pile, Loge adds the Tarnhelm to the booty. Alberich initially flares up in anger, then calms himself with the knowledge that he can use the ring to order Mime to make another Tarnhelm.

Thinking the ransom complete, Alberich expects to be freed, only to hear Wotan say, "A golden ring shows on your finger. To get your freedom, that must also be left with us." Alberich is stunned at this demand. He refuses, saying, "My life, but not the ring!" Wotan then tears the ring from Alberich's finger and puts it on his own. After this Loge unties Alberich, who rages at the gods and bitterly curses the ring:

Through the ring comes unlimited power.
Now let whoever owns it find death.
Let none rejoice owning the ring, or have a happy mind.
Care shall consume the one who possesses it. Fear be the
   bread he eats.
While envy shall gnaw at those who wish they did.
Lusting after the ring, no one shall find any profit or
   delight.

Alberich leaves as the giants approach with Freya to collect their pay. Fricka and other gods join Wotan and Loge. When they see Freya, they feel their joy and youth returning. The giants place Freya between their staves, one on each side of her; this serves as a measure of the gold they require. As the gods pile up the gold, Fafner presses the gold together, demanding that the chinks be filled. All the gold is used, and still some of Freya's hair shows, until Loge adds the Tarnhelm. Then Fasolt goes up to the hoard and sees Freya's eye through a crack. Fafner demands that this cranny be filled with the gold ring on Wotan's finger.

Wotan refuses. Fasolt pulls Freya from behind the hoard, saying he will keep her forever. Freya cries out for help. When the gods urge Wotan to give up the ring, he turns on them in wrath, saying, "Leave me alone! The ring stays with me!"

At this crucial moment, the scene darkens, and a bluish light glows, as Erda, the earth goddess, suddenly arises out of the mountainous ground, stretches out a warning hand to Wotan, and tells him to "yield the cursed ring!" Saying that "wretchedness, doom, and disaster" accompany it, she insists that he hear her.

When Erda tells Wotan, "All things that are, perish. A mournful day dawns for the gods," and sinks back into the earth, Wotan unsuccessfully tries to restrain her, saying, "Wait, let me hear more wisdom!" Erda's visitation plunges Wotan into deep thought, from which he rouses himself to give the giants the ring. Freya is finally free; the gold has paid for Valhalla.

Fafner now greedily packs most of the gold in his sack. Fasolt objects and insists that they share equally. Fafner refuses. They struggle over the ring, and Fasolt succeeds in getting possession of it, but only momentarily. Fafner strikes Fasolt with his staff, takes the ring from his brother's dying grasp, puts it into the sack, and resumes packing. Wotan watches, horrified at the quickness with which the curse that Alberich put on the ring was carried out.

Fricka reminds Wotan that the gleaming fortress castle is now his to occupy, although this gives him no joy. Gloomily, he realizes, "A dreadful price paid for that hall!"

The Rhinegold ends with Wotan and Fricka leading the other gods across a rainbow bridge to far-distant Valhalla. As they cross, the gods hear the Rhinemaidens mourning their lost gold.

The Quest for Power and Its Psychological Cost

THE RING OF NIBELUNG IS FORGED, FOUGHT OVER, AND cursed in *The Rhinegold*. As a symbol—or ring of power— it represents the "magical thing" that we can become so obsessed with having that it takes us over. It can be wealth, fame, power over others, security, status, knowledge, sex, or an addictive substance. Anything becomes a "ring of power" if we end up being willing to sacrifice everything else in ourselves and everyone else in our lives in order to obtain it. Anything that has so strong a hold on us and requires this high a price does indeed have a "curse" on it.

THE CYCLE BEGINS: ALBERICH AND POWER

Alberich renounces love to forge the ring of power. For him it is a "ring of revenge." He seeks power after giving up on receiving love and acceptance, which he initially innocently thinks available, desperately and futilely tries to grasp, and is ridiculed for trying. For the "Alberich" in us, having power over others is an effort to compensate and retaliate for abuse, rejection, and humiliation. This is part of the psychology of people who "identify with the aggressor": the child who wants love and is instead abused becomes in turn an abusive adult.

Rejection and exclusion are common childhood or adolescent experiences that are emotionally wounding. They make a person feel impotent and unlovable. Playground cruelty often compounds much deeper wounds, because the child who is ridiculed, rejected, neglected, or abused at home, is a member of a prejudiced-against minority group, or is in some way physically unacceptable by being too little, too fat, or "funny looking" has a greater susceptibility to becoming the scapegoat or the excluded one.

Children who are rejected feel that there is something wrong or ugly about them; they have a kinship with Alberich the Nibelung, who was "too dark and ugly" to play with the beautiful people. Such children may grow up to be successful adults in the eyes of others, yet still feel they are Nibelungs—little or fat or homely rejectables—underneath the image of power and sophistication that others see. For example, Gloria Steinem in *Revolution From Within* describes seeing herself on television and being shocked by the difference between her inner self-image as a "plump brunette from Toledo, too tall and much too pudding-faced, with a voice that felt constantly on the very edge of some unacceptable emotion," and "this thin, pretty, blondish woman of medium height who seemed confident, even blasé."

When rejection and ridicule come from the opposite sex in adolescence or young adulthood, the wound is to the sense of being attractive or potent as a sexual person. Whether a metaphor for the social swim, or the deeper meaning that equates water with emotions and feeling, Alberich was not in his element in the underwater realm of the Rhine. He did not know how to behave; he was too eager and needy. His behavior and experience were like those of the socially inept man who wants a girlfriend and reaches for first one and then another in a social setting where he is led on and then made fun of for his amorous efforts. He becomes filled with rage and humiliation if this happens; someday, when he has the upper hand, he may take revenge on other women for this.

When an abused child, a rejected adolescent, or a humiliated man is finally able to deny his desire for acceptance and love, he can become an "Alberich," a man obsessed with power and an abuser of others. He may be relatively secure only when in a position to dominate or humiliate someone else, which gives him a false and fragile sense of superiority. Lack of self-worth and experiences of devaluation, rejection, or abuse in childhood, coupled with a desire for revenge, make people prone to become like Alberich.

Although "Alberich" may not dominate our personality, there are "Nibelungs" in all of us. Each of us has qualities that were rejected by people that mattered to us, whose love we wanted. Whatever is rejected by others, especially when we were children, is likely to become unacceptable and shameful to us as well, and so we repress this part, consigning it to the "underground," which means it will be undeveloped and distorted—dwarflike. Whatever it is will continue to exist in our psyches and may have considerable hidden influence. For example, in dysfunctional families, a child may be punished for his or her sexuality, curiosity, independence, dependency, aggression, affection, or honest perceptions and as a result feel ashamed or afraid of having these feelings or instincts, which continue to exist but in a distorted, projected, or undeveloped form.

Once he has the ring of power, Alberich becomes a merciless tyrant who enslaves all of the dwarves. Abused and driven by his obsession for power, he makes the Nibelungs work night and day to build up his hoard of gold, with which he intends to extend his influence until he rules the world. Like Mime, the Nibelungs cringe in fear of Alberich and do his bidding.

THE RHINEGOLD

Mime is the skilled craftsman who made the Tarn-helm, a delicately wrought work. The skill of Mime and the other Nibelungs is exploited, valued only as it confers more power on Alberich. Once Alberich rules the Nibelungs, there is no time for the simple pleasures and slow-paced life that the Nibelungs once enjoyed. In much the same way, the Industrial Revolution changed the lives of people. Workers who once lived in villages and farms, now put in long hours at factories and in coal mines under miserable and unsafe conditions.

When I think of Alberich and the Nibelungs as an interior experience, I am reminded of the bleak inner life of a workaholic, who cannot relax, play, or enjoy the company of friends or family. Driven by the need to be productive at all times, he takes no pleasure in the work that consumes him and may punish and be critical of any inner impulses to do otherwise; an inner slave driver keeps him working.

The Nibelungs are driven by Alberich's obsession for gold, as is Alberich. His desire for power has made him greedy, unable to focus on anything except getting more gold, which he expects will gain him more power. Work accumulating wealth keeps an Alberich from feeling the awful feelings that go with the conviction that he is ugly and unlovable, just as addictions and obsessions keep us from feeling childhood pain and adult emptiness.

Alberich and Mime can be two sides of the same coin: an Alberich, when he abuses someone weaker, usually becomes a Mime when someone stronger has power over him. People who have been abused and rejected turn out like Alberich if they are driven by revenge and have the power to take out their anger and self-hatred on anyone weaker and less powerful. More often—especially if they have been made to feel inferior—abused people turn out like Mime and the other Nibelungs, obedient and afraid in the presence of authority, resentful underneath.

THE SEDUCTIVENESS OF POWER: WOTAN

Wotan is the chief god with the most power. He personifies the archetype of the king and sky god. Characteristically, it is important to Wotan that his will be done—in this case, that the giants build Valhalla as he envisions it. Wotan is a power-seeking and power-establishing archetype, facilitated by the ability to take decisive action, strategize, make alliances, and maintain emotional distance. The allure and seduction of power are strongest when Wotan is a major archetypal force in the psyche and culture.

Wotan rides his horse in the midst of thunderclouds, carrying a spear. Engraved on its shaft are contracts and agreements binding on Wotan and others. Wotan's will is restrained by law, a principle he established.

Wotan's desire for Valhalla as a monument to himself puts him in conflict with this principle. Wotan, who established order through binding agreements, enters a contract with the giants in bad faith when he promises them Freya in return for building Valhalla. Once power is achieved, monuments seem to follow. Contemporary Wotans are business titans who build tall buildings named after themselves. Whether built on the highest mountain or to be the highest structure, they promote inaccessibility and isolation at the top. Like Valhalla, which Wotan envisioned as a well-guarded fortress, these structures are built to provide security and enhance prestige. When a man disregards the costs of acquisition that will bankrupt him psychologically or financially, he is obsessed.

THE PRICE OF POWER: FREYA

Freya is the goddess of love, youth, and beauty, qualities that go together. Love is an eternal quality, which daily renews us and keeps us emotionally young. Beauty is in the eye of the beholder—seen through the eyes of love, whatever and whomever we behold are beautiful. With a heart that loves and an eye for beauty, we appreciate what we have and feel gratitude; thus we keep, even in old age, a child's sense of wonder and awe for the mysteries around us. When we have love, while we grow chronologically older, we stay young. Without love, as we age we can become weary and cynical, security minded, untrusting, and paranoid. When Alberich renounced love in order to have power, he gave up youthful innocence and attraction to beauty as well.

Wotan's agreement to give the giants Freya as payment reverberates through other patriarchal myths. Symbolically this is the same price that Agamemnon was willing to pay in the *Iliad:* in exchange for the winds that would take the Greek fleet that he commanded to Troy, Agamemnon was willing to sacrifice his daughter, Iphigenia. It also reminds us of Zeus's agreement to let Hades abduct his daughter Persephone into the underworld. To maintain or acquire power and prestige, male figures like Wotan in myth and fairy tales make symbolic choices that parallel real-life decisions made by men (and increasingly by women) that call for sacrificing their connection to feminine values and family bonds as well as giving up innocence and trust.

Trading Freya for Valhalla is also a metaphor for an interior choice that many men make. They trade away a youthful attitude and openness to life, love, and beauty. In exchange, they acquire a cynical attitude that they call realistic. They build monuments to themselves, concern themselves with security, and become rigid and conservative in their outlook. As they grow old, many power-seeking men become even more obsessed with having control, which power provides. This is especially so if underneath the facade of being a powerful Wotan, there is a "Nibelung," a rejected child who grew up feeling inadequate and unlovable and is terrified of becoming vulnerable.

RATIONALIZATION: LOGE AS TRICKSTER

Wotan says he made the agreement with the giants because he listened to Loge. Loge is a German version of the messenger god. Like Hermes and Mercury, Loge is a trickster and traveler with a characteristic quickness of movement, agility of mind, and facileness of word.

Loge is also an archetypal predisposition to think of the possibilities that abound, to assume nothing is fixed. He visits rather than establishes. In his getting around, he hears and sees many different ways of being, others communicate with him, and he trades information. As a trickster, he can see susceptibilities in others and play on them.

Looked at psychologically, the agreement has come about because Wotan feels that he is entitled to have what he wants or needs and looks to Loge to find a way out of any trouble that might come up later. He does not expect to have to pay up and does not intend to give the giants Freya. What we hear is familiar: it is the justification, rationalization, and denial of a credit addict in serious debt, as well as a fairly common expectation that many businessmen have of their lawyers. We are probably all familiar with people who unrealistically did not expect a day of reckoning until they found themselves in Wotan's situation, facing the consequences.

THE VOICE OF REALITY, AFFILIATION, AND ALARM: FRICKA

Fricka is Wotan's wife and the voice of reality, affiliation, and alarm. She tells him the truth of the situation, which he does not want to hear. She has feelings of distress about the cost of what he has done, which he has managed to put aside and not think about. She is concerned for Freya and for the effect the loss of Freya will have on the gods. Without Freya's apples, the immortals will lose their immortality, and the race of the gods will die. Wotan does not want to hear what Fricka has to say. When she persists, she comes across as a nag.

Fricka's role is that of Wotan's discounted other half. Her values get in the way of what he is doing. As an inner figure, "Fricka" can get in the way of an ambitious "Wotan." However, if both are heeded by the person in which these archetypes compete, then ambition is tempered by a regard for human cost.

In traditional marriages, each spouse gives up a potential half of themselves in order to create a whole between them. The husband goes into the world, his achievements and success accomplished for the both of them, while his wife takes on the relating function for the two and may even be referred to by him as his "better half." She takes the place of his anima, as his feminine, relationship-making half; she intercedes for him with their children, maintains friendships for the couple, and tells him how he is feeling. As a result, he does not develop the ability to be emotionally perceptive, just as she does not develop abilities necessary for success in the world if he does it all for them both.

Fricka is critical of Wotan for building Valhalla. However, Wotan notes that she had previously gone along with him, saying that she had wanted the big house, too. Fricka replies sadly that she did so only because she hoped it would keep him at home. Fricka acknowledges her previous complicity. The pattern of alternately overlooking and then being alarmed at the potential cost is what codependents do with addicts as they alternate between denial and reality.

Obsessions and addictions influence us to "listen to Loge," to disregard Wotan's principle of honorable agreements and avoid Fricka's voice of reality, affiliation, and alarm. While we can readily see the alcohol or drug addict, compulsive gambler, or shopping addict doing this, it is harder to see when power is the addiction, because the acquisition of power is viewed as desirable and a measure of success, a just reward for ambition, good investments, and hard work. The allure and seduction of power are tremendous.

Wotan is a stunning example of how mythology is a reflection of our own deep psychological and cultural issues. Whether Germanic, Greek, or contemporary American, as long as the culture is patriarchal, the story of Wotan will be instructive. Wotan reflects the psychology of men who seek to have power and status and strive to be in a superior position that allows them to demand obedience from others. On achieving success, they are not satisfied. On closer examination, they are not even secure, and so we see them seeking yet another status symbol or source of power.

There is a connection between Alberich and Wotan that Wotan later acknowledges (in *Siegfried*) when he refers to himself as "Light Alberich." Alberich renounces love for power once and for all in order to forge the ring.

Wotan's original agreement with the giants to trade Freya and her golden apples for Valhalla would have had a similar result. Wotan thought it was possible for him to possess his particular symbol of power and not pay the price. Alberich did not have such illusions—or hopes.

GREED AND THE RING OF POWER: FAFNER

Fasolt and Fafner, the contractors who build Valhalla, are the last of the giants. Once they are extinct, the skills and knowledge of building they have will disappear with them. Fafner covets owning the entire hoard of gold of which the ring is a part, and he kills his brother Fasolt for it, adding it to his booty. After this, he becomes isolated and obsessed with guarding his treasure. He never works creatively again and never has a companion. After Fafner murders his only important relationship, he becomes a recluse and a miser whose only objective in life is to guard his hoard.

Symbolically, brothers can represent two competing tendencies in one person: when the gentler brother, who believes in fairness and wants woman's beauty, is killed by the brother who is motivated by envy and greed, it means that these motives have taken over the personality. When this happens, the possibility of having companions, love, or fulfilling work is destroyed.

ELUSIVE SEXUAL POWER: THE RHINEMAIDENS

The Rhinemaidens are like alluring mermaids, who are half-human and half-fish. As symbols, they can represent women who act instinctively and unconsciously, which gives them power over men; or they can be inner images — anima figures — in men who project them indiscriminately on women that they pursue, promiscuously going from one to another.

A woman "Rhinemaiden" has a combination of attractive human and coldly inhuman qualities. She may appear warm and yet seem to have ice water in her veins, because she responds unconsciously, instinctively, and impersonally to draw a man to her and yet has no real feelings for him, which comes as a shock when he assumes she does but is rejected. When she is a maternal figure to a child, it is even more devastating and confusing. When she is the feminine aspect of a man, his attention and apparent intimacy are seductive and also false.

A Rhinemaiden is like an attractive woman who generates the emotions that swirl around her and does not feel responsible for their effect. She is also without compassion for the unrequited love, hurt, anger, and pathetic or desperate measures she may inspire. To be otherwise requires empathy and understanding, which she has not developed. A man who has developed these qualities usually recognizes her coldness and is not attracted.

In order for a "Rhinemaiden" to be the woman of his dreams, a man has to be as unconscious as she is: she is a woman who resembles his own undeveloped anima or inner feminine. He, in turn, like Alberich, may be powerfully drawn first to one woman and then to another and another. When this happens, every time he mistakes a woman for his anima, he falls in love anew, chasing after an image each time. The chase can become an obsession in pursuit of an illusion.

Lacking a consistent inner relationship to the feminine within himself, a man who projects his anima onto a series of women is fickle in his emotional attachments and moods. For example, a man who is usually logical and thick skinned may become maudlin or sentimental, thin skinned, or hurt when he gets into a mood; when the mood (or anima influence) passes, so do these feelings and sensitivity.

As C. G. Jung described, one function of the anima as an inner figure is to mediate between a man's ego and the collective unconscious. Through this feminine part of his own psyche, he can be drawn into emotional depths where "the Rhinegold" as a metaphor for the Self—an archetypal source of joy, numinosity, meaning—can be found. Alberich is in a position to see the Rhinegold only because he is attracted to the Rhinemaidens and has entered their erotic and magical realm. In this regard, they serve as his guides in the same way that falling in love with a woman upon whom the anima is projected may draw a man who has until that time lived on the surface into the depths, which can either be destructive to the personality if he becomes obsessed with love or jealousy, or expand and deepen it.

THE RHINEGOLD: THE SELF

Pure gold—Rhinegold—in the realm of feeling is imper-
sonal, beautiful, intense, mysterious, like the purity of
love that can be consciously contemplated only by a mys-
tic in a state of bliss. Like the Rhinegold in its original
state, this natural gold is hidden in our depths. It is an
inner source of meaning or numinosity that fills us with
joy whenever we from time to time sense or glimpse its
presence, but it is beyond our conscious grasp, a symbol of
the archetype of the Self, which Jung described. An experience of the Self is ineffable, a connection with something
greater than ourselves.

To forge Rhinegold into an instrument of power that
can be used to subjugate others is like tapping into this
inner source of divinity and corrupting it. Charismatic
and demonic leaders do this, and their followers become
slaves to their leader's obsession for power and wealth.
The Reverend James Jones, whose disciples followed him
to their deaths in Jonestown, was such a leader, as was
Hitler, who had an awesome mesmerizing aura at the
height of his power.

THE CURSE OF THE RING

In the last scene, Wotan and Loge bring Alberich up from
the underground depths, as we might bring something out

of awareness to mind and hold it captive until we can deal with what it represents. Alberich is a shadow figure, a symbol of the potential of renouncing love for power, as well as of sadistic and vengeful tendencies that are often hidden in the unconscious. Alberich is Wotan's shadow in particular.

The seduction of power overwhelms Wotan momentarily, when he takes the ring from Alberich and puts it on his own finger. It seduces him, and he refuses to give it up. Freya and all she represents are once more held in balance as the price of keeping the ring. It is a close call, prevented by the unexpected appearance of Erda. She warns Wotan that wretchedness, doom, and disaster lie in the ring and tells him to yield it, which he does.

Wotan heeds Erda and is determined to learn more from her. Erda is the earth goddess of wisdom, a mysterious figure who rises up out of the earth/rock and speaks to Wotan of what he must do in the present and what she sees coming in the future. She intrigues Wotan. He wants to know her and learn wisdom, and he tries unsuccessfully to keep her from sinking back into the earth. His encounter with her is crucial for his development. After she makes an appearance—or arises into consciousness and is heeded—Wotan becomes a more complex character.

The curse Alberich pronounces on the ring holds whenever acquiring power in any form becomes an obsession: there is never enough, and there is no peace of mind.

OBSESSION WITH POWER AND POLITICS:
ADOLF HITLER, SADDAM HUSSEIN,
JOSEPH P. KENNEDY

As I became familiar with *The Ring of the Nibelung*, the psychiatrist in me became intrigued by my knowledge that Hitler was fascinated by the *Ring* cycle and identified with it in some way. I knew that he was a major patron, that he had insisted that SS officers attend, and required that schoolchildren be exposed to these operas; all of which had caused me to be biased against Wagner and the *Ring*. I had assumed that it extolled Nazi goals and reflected Hitler's dreams of triumph and was surprised that to the contrary, Valhalla and Wotan go up in flames in the last act of *Twilight of the Gods*, reflecting the fate of the Third Reich and Hitler's own end; his charred remains were found in a burnt-out bunker.

There are clues that Hitler identified with Wotan. For example, I was told that when Hitler traveled incognito, he assumed the name of "Mr. Wolf," which was also one of Wotan's assumed names. In *The Valkyrie*, Wotan and his son Siegmund hunted together as "Wolf" and "Wolfcub."

Might Hitler's choice of the *Ring* cycle be precisely because it was his own story? Psychologists know that when people are asked to name their favorite fairy tale, they very often unconsciously choose the story that is a metaphor for their own life. While it's likely that Hitler saw himself as Wotan, he would be far more accurately cast as unloved and rejected Alberich the Nibelung, who forged a ring of revenge and sought to rule the world. Alice Miller in *For Your Own Good: Hidden Cruelty in Child-Rearing and the Roots of Violence,* describes Hitler as an abused, sadistically humiliated, illegitimate child, who as an adult would make millions of people suffer in his obsessive drive for power.

Saddam Hussein is a contemporary tyrant, who was terrorized and abused as a child and also grew up to be an Alberich with power over others. Once Alberich had forged the ring, he drove his people, the Nibelung dwarves, unmercifully to acquire more gold for him; in Iraq and in his invasion of Kuwait, Saddam did the same in his quest for more oil or "black gold." Raised by a fanatical step-father, whose harsh discipline and hatred shaped him (in the same way that we will learn that Alberich raised his son, Hagan), Saddam Hussein and countless others in the Middle East grow up seeking power as vengeance.

Joseph P. Kennedy, former United States Ambassador to England, who founded a dynasty to fulfill his ambition for power can also be seen as a combination of Wotan and Alberich. Stung by social rejection because he was an Irish immigrant, he was motivated to acquire power to get revenge for his humiliation. For Kennedy, the presidency of the United States was the "ring of power." To fulfill his obsession, his sons Joseph Jr., John, and Robert went after it; just as we will see in subsequent operas that the sons of Wotan and Alberich were conceived as a means to acquire possession of the ring of power for their fathers.

The quest for power is not just instilled in men who seek revenge for their own or their fathers' humiliations or ambitions. Power is what is valued most in patriarchal systems of all kinds, and when power matters more than love, there are terrible consequences, which is what *The Ring of the Nibelung* tells us.

BRUNNHILDE *implores Wotan to reconsider. When power is the ruling principle rather than love, a relationship is expendable if it is no longer useful, and disobeying authority can be severely punished. To respond with compassion, feminine values need to be heeded.*

THE VALKYRIE
(DIE WALKÜRE)

THE AUTHORITARIAN
FATHER AND THE
DYSFUNCTIONAL FAMILY

CAST OF CHARACTERS

THE MORTALS

Siegmund: *son of Wotan and an unnamed mortal woman; twin brother of Sieglinde*

Sieglinde: *Siegmund's twin sister, who becomes his lover*

Hunding: *Sieglinde's husband*

THE IMMORTALS

Wotan: *chief god; father of Siegmund and Sieglinde (the Walsungs) and Brunnhilde*

Fricka: *goddess of marriage; wife of Wotan*

Brunnhilde: *"the Valkyrie"; daughter of Wotan and Erda, one of the nine Valkyries*

Valkyries: *nine immortal virgin warrior daughters of Wotan, who ride magic horses through the storm clouds of war and bring dead heroes who fall in battle to Valhalla; Waltraute, Gerhilde, Ortlinde, Schwertleite, Helmwige, Siegrune, Grimgerde, Rossweise, and Brunnhilde*

CHAPTER 2

THE VALKYRIE

The Authoritarian Father and the Dysfunctional Family

The Story

AN EXHAUSTED MAN COMES OUT OF A RAGING STORM INTO A house. He finds himself alone, and collapses on the hearth in an unusual room built around the trunk of a huge ash tree that rises through the roof. Sieglinde, the woman of the house, hears him. Thinking that it is her husband Hunding returning, she enters the room and is surprised to see a stranger lying by the fire. It is Siegmund, who stirs, opens his eyes, and gazes at her. When their eyes meet, they are both powerfully attracted to each other.

Revived, and hearing that she expects her husband to return shortly, Siegmund goes to the door and lifts the latch to leave, explaining that he must go because "misfortune follows my footsteps," misfortune that he does not want to bring to her. She insists that he stay, telling him that misfortune has long been with her.

When Hunding returns, the three sit down to dinner. Hunding is astonished at the resemblance between the two, noting that they both have an unusual shine in their eyes as well. When he is asked who he is, Siegmund calls himself "Woeful"

45

and explains that he is named for his sorrow: one day when he was a youngster, he and Wolf, his father, came back from a day of hunting to find their home burned, his mother murdered, and his twin sister missing. He and his father then lived in the woods, hunting together, as Wolf and Wolfcub, until one day the raiders came again. Father and son fought well and fled. In the flight they were separated. When he searched for his father, he found only the wolfskin that he had worn. Since then, every effort he has made to be with people has been met with rejection. Whatever he thinks is right others consider wrong; what seems bad to him others call good. Consequently, he has always been "Woeful," and sadness has been his fate.

Most recently, he had come to the aid of a woman who was being forced to marry a man she feared by her brothers. Hearing her cry, he had intervened and was attacked by them. He then killed all her brothers, and she became grief stricken. Then her brothers' kinsmen rushed to the fight. He protected her with his sword and shield until they were shattered, and she was killed. Then he fled.

Hunding is disturbed by the story and announces that the men Siegmund killed were his kin. Though he will honor hospitality to Wolfcub for the night, Hunding tells him that he had better find some weapons, for in the morning he will fight him. He orders Sieglinde to prepare his drink for the night and to come to their bedchamber.

Siegmund is alone, unarmed in the house of his enemy, with his heart open to this lovely woman. He remembers that his father promised him a sword in an hour of need, and he calls out, "Walse! Walse! Where is your sword, your shining sword that can save me?" In that instant, a place on the ash tree where Sieglinde silently directed her eyes before leaving the room glows brightly.

Later that night, after the fire has burned out, Sieglinde comes to Siegmund. She has drugged Hunding's drink, and now, embracing Siegmund, she tells him that there is a sword buried in the ash tree and how it came to be there. On the day of her wedding, Hunding and his relatives had gathered in this room. He had married her against her will, and it was an unhappy occasion for her. Then a stranger entered the house. "An old man dressed all in gray. His hat hung so low that one of his eyes was hidden. A threatening glance from the other eye filled the men with terror. I alone saw that there were sorrow and solace in his gaze. He carried a sword in his hand, which he drove deeply into the ash tree, burying it to the hilt."

Sieglinde explains that after the old man left, every man there, all of them warriors, tried to draw the sword from the tree, but none could budge it. It is the hilt of this sword that glows.

The darkened room suddenly becomes illuminated by the light from a full moon, allowing the embracing couple to see each other clearly. Enraptured, each sees himself or herself in the beloved face of the other. In their glances, both also recognize a certain gleam by which Sieglinde says that she recognized the old man in gray as her father. Siegmund recalls his father, "Walse," whose eyes shone on him, as Sieglinde's does now. In this moment of clarity, they know who they are to each other. The sword is the proof. Promised a sword by his father in his hour of need, here is the sword that was placed there by her father. Siegmund grasps the hilt, names the sword "Notung" ("Needful"), and calls upon it to come to him. Then, with a great pull, he draws the sword from the tree, shows it to Sieglinde, and claims her as his sister and bride.

WOTAN AND FRICKA

In the mountains, Wotan anticipates the battle between Hunding and Siegmund with great enthusiasm. He is armed and carries his spear, and he exhorts his daughter the Valkyrie Brunnhilde to bridle her horse, take up her shield, and be off with him to the fight. He tells her the outcome: "Siegmund the Walsung is victor today! Hunding falls to him!" Brunnhilde is to leave him where he lies, however, since Wotan does not consider Hunding fit to be taken to Valhalla. Brunnhilde responds with exuberance, but before they can leave, she sees Fricka, Wotan's wife, approaching.

Fricka arrives in her chariot, and rather than storm at him, which Wotan expects, she addresses him with dignity. She is there "to claim the help you owe me." She has come on Hunding's behalf to seek his victory over Siegmund. Describing herself as "wedlock's guardian" (like the Greek goddess Hera), Fricka herself has sworn to punish the deed.

"But what evil have they done?" Wotan asks. "The power of love overcame them both; who could resist that power?" Sieglinde and Siegmund broke holy vows, Fricka maintains. Wotan counters, saying that he calls "the vows that bind unloving hearts unholy."

Fricka sarcastically suggests that he might then praise as holy the incest that Siegmund and Sieglinde have committed. The idea that a brother and sister are lovers shocks and offends her. Wotan retorts that she has something to learn from this — that a thing may happen that has never happened before, and that Siegmund and Sieglinde love each other, as she must know. Fricka then blames Wotan for having forgotten the race of gods, for betraying his faithful wife and breaking her heart. Even so, she notes that he has continued to treat her with respect and has bound the Valkyries, including Brunnhilde, to be obedient to her. She tells him that matters worsened when he took the name "Walse," prowled through the woodland like a wolf, and had a common woman bear his children. But he will "stoop to the depth of dishonor" if for these "whelps" he now abandons his wife.

Wotan tells Fricka that she is missing the point. Siegmund is the hero who is free of the gods and thus can accomplish a deed that would save them, for he can do that which the gods

THE VALKYRIE

themselves are forbidden to do: he can obtain the ring of the Nibelung. Fricka thinks Wotan is just making up a new excuse to save Siegmund. She also disagrees with his premise that Siegmund could be this free hero: "In him I find only you; what he does, he does through you." Wotan denies that this is so, saying, "In wildest sorrow, he grew by himself, and I gave him no help."

"Then do not help him now! Take back the sword you placed in his hand," she replies, "the magical, glittering sword that the god has given his son!"

When Wotan insists that Siegmund won it himself, Fricka disputes him point by point: it was Wotan who sent him the sword and his need for it. It was Wotan who promised it to him, who made it, put it in the tree, and led him to it. After concluding that far from being a free hero, Siegmund is Wotan's servant, she asks, "Must I be subjected to him?" Will Wotan "allow me, his goddess, to suffer this shame?"

Wotan is backed into a corner by Fricka's words and, in a poignant dialogue, concedes point by painful point that he will abandon Siegmund, that he will give him no help, that he will command Brunnhilde that Siegmund is to die, and that he will break the magic sword.

WOTAN AND BRUNNHILDE

After Fricka departs, Brunnhilde returns to find Wotan brooding. When she asks him what troubles him, he is full of self-pity. He describes himself as unfree and the saddest of beings. It is hard for him to tell her why he is upset, for he fears he will lose power over her if he does. Brunnhilde reminds him that she is there to do what he wills. There are tenderness and intimacy between them as he confides in her.

Wotan tells her about events that happened before she was born and about the ring of the power he seeks to own. It began when love vanished, and he sought power, listened to Loge, and contracted with the giants to build Valhalla. In the meantime, Alberich forged the ring of power by renouncing love, something Wotan could not do because "the longing for love would not leave me." He confessed that he stole the ring from Alberich and used it to buy Valhalla after Erda warned him not to keep the ring and predicted doom for the gods. Then, feeling a compelling need to learn more from Erda, he conquered her "by love's enchantment." Erda then gave birth to Brunnhilde, who with her eight sister Valkyries are assembling an army of heroes to guard Valhalla. Wotan fears Alberich, knowing that envy and rage burn in him and that if Alberich were to repossess the ring, he would use it to conquer Valhalla.

After Fafner the giant killed his brother Fasolt over the ring, Fafner turned himself into a dragon who now guards the gold and the ring. As a consequence of the contract he made with the giants, Wotan is in a bind. He must have the ring of power, yet he cannot harm Fafner and take it from him.

He explains to Brunnhilde that his solution was a free hero, who on his own accord, with no prompting or aid from Wotan, could kill Fafner and get the ring. This was to be Siegmund's role and why Wotan had provided him with the magic sword. But the plan has come to nothing. He has deluded himself—as Fricka has made him see—to think Siegmund was free. Wotan now concludes that he has no power to make a free person, that his hand can make only slaves. Meanwhile, he has heard that Alberich has bought a woman's embrace with gold, and she will bear his son, a birth that Wotan fears will fulfill Erda's prophecy, signaling the end of the gods.

Finally, Wotan tells Brunnhilde that Siegmund must die: "Though I loved him, I must abandon him. I will murder the son I love and betray him when he trusts me!" Wotan tells Brunnhilde that she must be Fricka's champion and fight for Hunding. Brunnhilde is shocked, and she begs Wotan to let his love for Siegmund command her instead, which he refuses to do. Brunnhilde tells Wotan that he has taught her to love Siegmund, and that if he asks her to kill him, she will refuse.

Wotan reacts with fury: "Do what I say! What are you but the obedient blind slave of my will?" He warns Brunnhilde not to rouse his wrath, which could lay waste to all the world. Stunned by his rage, Brunnhilde sorrowfully accepts his command: Hunding is to be the victor; Siegmund is to die.

BRUNNHILDE'S ACT OF COMPASSION AND DISOBEDIENCE

When Brunnhilde first sees Siegmund and Sieglinde, they are in a mountain pass. Sieglinde is distraught and distressed and rushes ahead of Siegmund, who calls after her to stop. Finally, when she is too tired to continue her flight, he catches up with her. After they made love, she had fled in fear and frenzy. He holds her now and asks her to trust him, promising that he will shelter her from harm.

Sieglinde gazes at Siegmund in rapture and passionately returns his embrace. Then, in sudden terror, she tells him to fly away from her, calling herself unholy, cursed, disgraced, dishonored, and dead in her heart. She tells him to cast her away, to fling her aside. She is in great turmoil and conflict, overwhelmed by an upwelling of contradictory feelings. She tells him that when they made love she found such blissful delight that all of her love was awakened, and she had responded to him with all her soul and senses, only to find that this evoked loathing and horror. She is close to madness as she now calls herself a traitorous woman whom Hunding owned as wife, without honor or grace, who because of her guilt must abandon her purest hero because of the shame she would bring to him.

Then they hear the sound of horns, of men and dogs pursuing them. Sieglinde is terrified, sobs, and seems to lose touch with reality. She no longer sees Siegmund, who is holding her.

RING OF POWER

Instead she is gazing at a horrifying vision that she describes: dogs are leaping at Siegmund's throat and pulling him down. His shining sword is in splinters. Crying out to Siegmund, she faints in his arms.

Siegmund gently eases Sieglinde to the ground and cradles her head in his lap. He is in this position when Brunnhilde appears to him holding her spear and leading her horse. When he wonders who she is, she tells him that only those doomed to death can see her: she is here to lead him to Valhalla, where he will be welcomed by Wotan, other fallen heroes, and fair maidens. He asks her whether his father, Walse, is there; she replies that his father waits to greet him.

Then Siegmund asks whether she has come for Sieglinde as well. Brunnhilde tells him, "No"; he will have to leave her behind. On hearing this, Siegmund tells Brunnhilde to greet them all—Wotan, Walse, heroes, and maidens—for him. He will not go.

Brunnhilde informs Siegmund that Hunding will kill him and the sword that his father gave him will not protect him. "Then shame on him who bestowed the sword," Siegmund says to her, and he vows that though he dies he will not go to Valhalla. Brunnhilde is shocked and asks incredulously, "You would sacrifice everlasting joy? You would leave Valhalla for her?"

Siegmund bitterly tells Brunnhilde not to mock him. Calling her heartless and cruel, he tells her to leave him alone. "If it delights you to watch my woe, you're free to feed on my pain, but of Valhalla's loveless pleasures, you need tell me no more."

Brunnhilde is deeply affected by Siegmund's love and grief. She tells him that she feels all of his suffering and pain, and she promises, "I'll care for your wife. I'll shield her safely from harm."

Siegmund rejects this too. He tells Brunnhilde that so long as Sieglinde lives, he will allow no one else to touch her, and if he has to die, he will kill Sieglinde first while she sleeps.

THE VALKYRIE

Brunnhilde calls him a madman, reiterates that she will shield and care for his wife, and tells him that a son shall be born from his love. Siegmund does not listen to her and instead draws his sword. Telling her that since he now knows it will fail him in a fight, he will use it instead on a friend.

Brunnhilde finds that she can no longer carry out Wotan's command to see that Siegmund dies. Moved by compassion, she decides to act on her own and disobey Wotan. She promises Siegmund that she will join him in battle, his sword will be true, and he and Sieglinde will live together.

Sieglinde is sleeping peacefully as Siegmund gently lays her down and kisses her farewell. Then, drawing his sword, he leaves to fight Hunding. Sieglinde now stirs restlessly. She is dreaming and cries out in her sleep: "Why doesn't father return? He is still in the woods with the boy. Mother! Mother! I feel afraid—they seem unfriendly; who are the strangers?! They burn the house! Oh, help me, brother! Siegmund! Siegmund!" Awakening, she looks around in terror and finds herself in the midst of thunder and lightning. She hears Hunding's horn, Siegmund and Hunding's voices, and then the sound of fighting.

As the two men fight, Brunnhilde appears in a blaze of light above Siegmund. She protects him and urges him to strike Hunding with his sword. Just as Siegmund is about to strike a deadly blow, Wotan is suddenly standing over Hunding; his spear shatters Siegmund's sword, allowing Hunding to plunge his blade into Siegmund's chest, killing him. In that instant, Brunnhilde turns to Sieglinde, lifts her on her horse, and disappears with her.

The scene ends with Wotan gazing sadly on Siegmund's body before contemptuously telling Hunding, "Go! Go! Tell Fricka that Wotan's spear avenged her cause of shame." Wotan waves his hand, and Hunding falls dead to the ground. Now Wotan rages against Brunnhilde, whom he calls "the guilty one."

RING OF POWER

BRUNNHILDE RESCUES SIEGLINDE

The Valkyries are gathering on a mountain summit. Each sings out her call, as they welcome one another. Their horses are fresh from battle and are still spirited. Comments go back and forth about their horses or are made to their horses. Each is bringing a dead hero to Valhalla, and they inquire of one another, "Who hangs from your saddle?" The feeling is that of a successful hunt; there is a postvictory, locker-room camaraderie, as each Valkyrie is accounted for until there are eight. Only Brunnhilde is missing.

From a lookout point, one of the Valkyries sees Brunnhilde coming. She rides furiously and has driven her horse, Grane, to the point of exhaustion. They had expected her to be coming with the body of Siegmund. Instead they see that her horse is carrying a young woman. She arrives on the scene breathless with exertion, supporting and leading Sieglinde, and calls out to them, "Shield me and help me!" To them, Brunnhilde appears to be in desperate flight, which she confirms: "I flee for the first time. I am pursued. Wotan is hunting me!"

The Valkyries think Brunnhilde mad to have defied Wotan. "How could you!" is their initial response. She asks each sister in turn for her horse that she might save Sieglinde from Wotan's wrath, and each sister in turn denies her this help. Meanwhile, Sieglinde wants no part of this. With Siegmund dead, she longs only for death, until Brunnhilde tells Sieglinde that she is carrying Siegmund's child. At this news, Sieglinde's face lights up in rapture. "Save me, you maidens, and shelter my son!" she now implores the Valkyries. Her pleas fall on deaf ears. On her knees, she pleads to Brunnhilde, "Rescue me, maid! Rescue a mother!"

Brunnhilde is moved by Sieglinde's words and feelings. Once again, her compassion directs her course of action, this time to save Sieglinde and her unborn son. Brunnhilde tells Sieglinde that she will be safe from Wotan's wrath if she flees by herself toward a gloomy forest where Fafner the dragon has his cave. It is a place "Wotan fears and never goes near." Brunnhilde will stay behind. "I will brave Wotan's anger and draw his revenge on myself, so that you can escape his rage."

As Wotan approaches, Brunnhilde gives Sieglinde the pieces of Siegmund's shattered sword and sees her off safely, foreseeing the difficulties she is to face. Sieglinde will have to endure hunger, thirst, thorns, and stones. However, she will be able to laugh at the pain and grief, knowing that "Siegfried," "the noblest hero of all," shall be born from her womb. She is to take the broken pieces of Siegmund's sword so that their son can forge a new sword from the fragments.

WOTAN'S WRATH AT BRUNNHILDE

Sieglinde gets safely away before Wotan arrives in a towering rage. The Valkyries retreat up the mountain, hiding Brunnhilde in their midst. They try to intervene on her behalf and ask Wotan to "have mercy on her, calm your dreadful rage," which has the opposite effect of provoking him into a tirade against themselves and Brunnhilde. At the heart of his wrath toward her is his accusation that "she has broken the bond of our love and faithless defied my desire" by going against his command. Finally, he thunders, "Hear me, Brunnhilde! You whom I fashioned, you who owe all that you are, name, even life, to me! Can you hear me accuse you, and hide yourself to try to escape your doom! You coward!"

At this, Brunnhilde steps out from the midst of her sisters and resolutely yet humbly walks toward Wotan. "Here I am, Father," she says. "Tell me my sentence."

Wotan tells Brunnhilde she has brought her doom on herself, and once more he angrily enumerates her sins of disobedience against him. He ends by pronouncing, "Though once you were all that I made you, what you have become you chose for yourself! No more, child of my will; you are a Valkyrie no longer. Henceforth, remain what you chose to be!" "No more will you ride from Valhalla; no more shall you fill drinking horn for me; no more may I kiss the mouth of my child." She is to be "cast forever from the clan of the gods."

Brunnhilde's eight Valkyrie sisters react with dismay as Wotan tells Brunnhilde what her fate will be. He will put her into a deep sleep, so that she will be utterly defenseless. She will belong to the first man who finds her and awakens her. "The flower of her beauty will fade and die. A husband will gain all her womanly grace; that masterful husband will make her obey. She will sit and spin by the fire, and all the world will deride her fate!"

As the Valkyries shrink in horror at what Wotan has decreed, they are told that if any one of them should dare to come by and console Brunnhilde, that rash one will share her fate. Furthermore, they are to ride away immediately and not go near her now, or the same fate shall be theirs.

WOTAN PUNISHES BRUNNHILDE

After the Valkyries have left in haste and distress, the storm subsides, and the thunderclouds disperse, which of course is a reflection of Wotan's emotional state. There is calm; Wotan and Brunnhilde are alone. He is seated; she lies at his feet.

Brunnhilde raises her head and asks Wotan softly and persistently whether her offense was so shameful, so disgraceful, so dishonorable, so boundless, so base that she deserves to be shamed, dishonored, and abandoned. She speaks to him gently and solicitously, as women do with a powerful man who can at any moment become abusive. Gradually, she raises herself to a kneeling position and asks him to look into her eyes, soften his anger, and explain why he is punishing her so terribly.

THE VALKYRIE

Wotan tells Brunnhilde bitterly that she understood his order perfectly and had been warned by him of his rage if she failed to carry out his will. "But no, you thought: Wotan is weak!" Brunnhilde does not respond directly to this accusation; instead she shifts the focus: "I know so little, but one thing I did know: you loved Siegmund. I saw all your torment as you tried to force yourself to forget this."

Brunnhilde then explains why she shielded Siegmund, not to defy Wotan or because she thought him weak but because of what happened when she appeared to take him to Valhalla: "I said you had marked him for death. I gazed in his eyes then and heard his reply. I felt this hero's grief and distress and witnessed his courage." She tells Wotan that what she had perceived with her eyes and heard with her ears troubled and affected her. "A new emotion stole through my heart." She was astonished and shamed by Siegmund's loyalty and love for Sieglinde and wanted to help and save him.

Wotan responds bitterly to Brunnhilde's explanations, telling her that she indulged her love, that it had led her away from him, and that his terrible rage was awakened by terrible grief. He contrasts himself with her: "To save creation," he imprisoned "the spring of love in his tortured heart," while she "lay lapped in blissful delight, filled with emotion's rapturous joy." Wotan's accusations are distortions that reveal his jealousy.

Each time Brunnhilde speaks, she risks provoking Wotan. Though she is to be stripped of her immortality and cruelly abandoned by him, he is the one who expresses his feelings of betrayal. When she tries to explain her actions, he reacts like a spurned lover. The issue seems to be no longer her defiance of his authority but her unfaithfulness to him. Thus when she asks Wotan to at least "be sure no craven braggart makes me his prize; be sure some hero wins me as bride!" he replies, "You turned away from Wotan; your conqueror I cannot choose." She will be exposed and sexually available to the first man who comes upon her and thus becomes her master.

RING OF POWER

Brunnhilde tells Wotan that by abandoning her, "You abandon half of your being. That other self, you must not disgrace." "Your fame then would be darkened, if I were scorned and despised."

Wotan spurns these appeals. Nor is he moved when Brunnhilde tells him that by saving Sieglinde, she saved the Walsung race. Instead he blames their doom on her. "By your desertion of me, the Walsungs were doomed. My rage destroys all the race!"

All Brunnhilde's efforts to soften Wotan's anger or her punishment seem to fall on a hardened heart. He is vehement when he tells her, "Seek not, oh, child, to change my decision!" "I have been delayed here too long. For as you turned from me, I turn from you." "I must now see your sentence fulfilled!"

"What have you decreed that I must suffer?" Brunnhilde asks.

"In long, deep sleep you shall be bound. The man who wakes you makes you his wife," he tells her.

Brunnhilde is anguished and pleads with Wotan that if she is to be left unconscious, a prize for the first man who comes upon her, let him at least be a fearless, free hero. Wotan replies that she is asking for too great a grace.

Hearing this, she clings to Wotan's legs and begs him to kill her at once. "Let my breast receive one blow from your spear. Cast not this shame, this cruel disgrace on me!"

In the next moment, as if she has received a sudden inspiration, Brunnhilde tells Wotan that he can command a ring of fire to surround the rock on which she is to lie asleep that will stop a coward from approaching her.

In response, Wotan raises Brunnhilde from her knees, gazes into her eyes, and sings a passionate farewell to her, promising that "a bridal fire shall blaze to protect you. The cowardly will cringe, the weak will flee from Brunnhilde's rock. One alone wins you as bride, one freer than I, the god!"

THE VALKYRIE

Hearing this, Brunnhilde joyfully throws herself into Wotan's arms, and he holds her in a long embrace. Looking tenderly at her, he movingly speaks of her radiant, glorious eyes that he often kissed, that shone so brightly in the storm, that gladdened him when he was fearful or yearned for worldly pleasures. "Their glorious fire gladdens me now, as I take this loving, last farewell! On some happy mortal one day they will shine, but I, hapless immortal, must lose them forever."

Wotan holds Brunnhilde's head in his hands, and saying, "My kiss takes your godhead away," kisses her on her eyes. Brunnhilde falls unconscious in his arms. He lays her down, closes her helmet, and covers her with her great shield.

Now Wotan takes his spear and strikes the point of it against the rock three times, calling upon Loge, the god of fire. "Arise! Come, flickering Loge! Surround the rock, ring it with flame!" The fire comes. With his spear, Wotan directs it so it encircles the mountain on which Brunnhilde lies asleep. As if casting a spell, Wotan then stretches out his spear, saying prophetically, "Only the man who braves my spearpoint can pass through this sea of flame."

The Psychology of Power in the Dysfunctional Family

THE VALKYRIE FOCUSES ON RELATIONSHIPS THAT RE-flect what we see in dysfunctional families headed by a powerful, authoritarian man. In them, as in most dysfunctional relationships, what happens between people is decided by the power one person has over the other rather than by the love between them, even when there is love.

In *The Valkyrie*, marriages are patriarchal or traditional. The husband has power over his wife and over the form their marriage will take. There are incestuous relationships between parent and child and between siblings, codependent behavior, infidelity, narcissism, and suffering as well as moments of truth and acts of compassion and courage.

The psychological roles in *The Valkyrie* reflect those in real-life dysfunctional families. There are the authoritarian father (Wotan) and husband (Wotan, Hunding), the discounted and angry wife (Fricka) or the passive and obedient wife (Sieglinde), the powerless or absent mother (nameless mother of Sieglinde and Siegmund, Erda), and emotionally abandoned and abused children (Siegmund, Sieglinde) or children who are expected to fulfill the emotional needs or ambitions of a parent (Brunnhilde, Siegmund).

DYSFUNCTIONAL MARRIAGES

There are two marriages in *The Valkyrie*. In both, the husband is master of the house and has the upper hand. Hunding and Sieglinde's marriage is lawful, patriarchal marriage at its worst, unsoftened by affection from the very beginning. Sieglinde is Hunding's property; she and the house belong to him. She was married against her will and, once married, does what Hunding wants. There is no one she can go to for support, and no place to go to for shelter. Through marriage, her material needs and her social role are secured. What she feels or wants does not matter.

Hunding is a man who successfully fits into his milieu, an example of patriarchal society. He has a dutiful wife and a house, kinship alliances that he can count on for reciprocated aid, a place in the world, and rules to live by. In marked contrast to Siegmund, personal feelings, either his own or those of others, are not important. Hunding can marry a woman against her will; he can demand and expect her to take care of the house and his needs, including sexual ones. He can let a man be a guest overnight because a rule of hospitality has been invoked and kill him in the morning, because the guest is an enemy of his kin. Maintaining the form is what matters to Hunding. He lives within the law and can call upon allies and deities—the system—to avenge him.

WOTAN AND FRICKA:
PORTRAIT OF A DYSFUNCTIONAL MARRIAGE

Wotan and Fricka are also in a dysfunctional patriarchal marriage. However, there was once love between them. Either love left and Wotan sought power, or love left when he sought power; in either case, love has gone. On hearing that an angry Fricka is approaching, Wotan remarks, "The usual storm, the usual strife." Theirs is a marriage that endures in form but is empty of intimacy and love. Fricka is resentful and angry, which prevents her from feeling or dwelling on her pain and betrayal. Wotan has had numerous extramarital relationships and has fathered many children who are adults in *The Valkyrie*. He has left Fricka emotionally, yet he maintains the marriage and insists that she be treated with the respect due her as his wife.

This is a fairly common dysfunctional marriage pattern for men who are archetypally like Wotan (or Zeus) with wives like Fricka (or Hera). The institution of marriage is important to such a man as a source of stability and status, as it is for the woman, especially if her meaning and identity are derived from being married to him.

Hostility toward one another and mutual depression are present in such marriages, and these feelings take their toll on the couple and on the family. In loveless marriages, power becomes a substitute for love: it is as if each decides "if I can't get love, I'll get my way." Anger or intimidation through the threat of it, holding onto the purse strings, and withholding sex are common ways in which one spouse expresses power over the other. In some actively dysfunctional marriages, there are ongoing power struggles and outward expressions of hostility, with temporary winners and stalemates. In other dysfunctional marriages, passive acceptance of the status quo is the pattern, and hostility goes underground. In either case, the lack of love and affirmation is a source of insecurity and emotional pain, predisposing husband and wife to addictive behavior that numbs the pain, or physical or psychological symptoms that express it indirectly.

FRICKA AS THE BETRAYED WIFE
AND UPHOLDER OF MARRIAGE

Fricka calls herself "wedlock's guardian." In this, she is the equivalent to Hera, the Greek goddess of marriage, for whom marriage was holy and sacred, a divine bond. Fricka is wounded by Wotan's infidelities, as was Hera, whose husband, Zeus, was a philanderer. For Fricka, Hera, and ordinary women who have the same deep archetypal sense of marriage, infidelity is an evil. When marriage bonds are broken, that which they hold most sacred is desecrated, and a source of deep personal meaning is destroyed. They react with outrage and want the infidelity to be avenged. Dependent as they are on their unfaithful husbands, they may displace their revenge onto others. Fricka's demand that Hunding be avenged through Siegmund's death is an expression of this displacement.

Anger and vengeance keep the betrayed spouse from feeling the deep grief and powerlessness she would otherwise feel. Holding onto appearances and the prerogatives of being the wife of a powerful man hide her humiliation from herself and others. Substituting acquisition of material possessions for love keeps the emotional impoverishment at a distance, while power over others expressed in a punitive way may keep her from feeling helpless, worthless, and abandoned. Substance abuse, most commonly alcohol, helps numb these feelings that she cannot bear. The neglected wives of powerful men are susceptible to becoming caught up in one or more of these behaviors.

FRICKA AS THE VOICE OF REALITY

In *The Valkyrie*, as in *The Rhinegold*, Fricka is Wotan's voice of reality who confronts his self-delusions. Once again, Wotan is trying to get around the agreement that he made with the giants to build Valhalla years before. This time, he does not blame Loge or expect Loge to handle his problem for him. Psychologically, "Loge" is no longer an outside influence but is instead a devious way of thinking Wotan does himself. Thus Wotan devises a long-range plan to get the ring of power that ostensibly will not involve him but will be done by a "free hero."

Fricka can represent the discounted and repressed voice of reality and of fidelity that results when obsessive (or addictive) drives motivate anyone. When someone is obsessed, fidelity to values, loyalty to people, clear thinking, and good judgment are often lost or rationalized away.

The need to possess power is justified by Wotan as necessary in order to save the gods, a rationalization that attempts to make his personal obsession serve a higher good, which political Wotans have always done. When either an inner or an outer voice cautions against this course, that voice becomes a resented nag, at best, or a traitor to be silenced.

WOTAN AS A NARCISSISTIC PARENT

Confronted by Fricka's demand that Hunding be avenged and Siegmund die, Wotan explains that Siegmund was conceived for the sole purpose of getting the ring Wotan covets and that an orphaned Siegmund grew up "in wildest sorrow" by himself, in order that he be ostensibly unhelped and uninfluenced by Wotan and thus a "free hero," which Wotan sees as a solution to his problem of getting the ring without breaking his agreement. Siegmund has to suffer a terrible childhood and be an outcast in order to become the means through which Wotan can get the ring of power.

In psychological terms, Wotan is a narcissistic parent. As far as he is concerned, Siegmund exists only to further his need for power. Thus Siegmund is not loved, nurtured, or seen as a child with the right to have his own needs met and find his own purpose in life. Wotan can abandon Siegmund to lead a woeful life because it serves his purpose and can agree that Siegmund must die when Wotan's plan does not work. After this, Wotan feels sorry for himself, bemoaning that he is "the saddest of beings" because his plan has failed. He feels nothing for Siegmund, since he sees the situation only from his own perspective.

For personal and dynastic reasons, men like Wotan often seek to have sons: to carry on the family name or business, to be the successful athlete, political figure, or whatever the father aspired to be and now can live out through a son. When this is a family pattern, to keep his parent's approval, a child learns to suppress his own feelings and contrary inclinations and grows up not feeling loved for himself.

When a father is narcissistic, if a beloved daughter disobeys him, disagrees with him, or leaves him to live her own life, he may react as if she is betraying him. He cannot see her as a separate being with her own needs to be met or see that her best interests might not be the same as his own, which makes him unable to be a genuinely caretaking parent. (This also applies to narcissistic mothers and their children.) The child is put in the position of having to abandon parts of herself and her needs for growth in order to keep the relationship with the parent.

A narcissistic person lacks empathy and cannot put himself in another's position. He or she also has an inordinate amount of rage under the surface, which is evident in Wotan. The closeness between Wotan and Brunnhilde shifts alarmingly when she says that if he asks her to kill Siegmund, she will refuse. The idea that she could disobey him makes Wotan furious, and he warns her that her disobedience will unleash his destructive wrath. He is making her responsible for keeping him out of a rage, a function commonly accepted by others as their responsibility in a dysfunctional family.

Because of his need for control, Wotan expects Brunnhilde to be a codependent when he demands obedience and expects her to abandon her own feelings as well as to abandon Siegmund. Narcissists make codependents of their children and of anyone else who will put the narcissist's needs before their own. When Wotan tells Brunnhilde that if she disobeys him, then she (rather than he) will be responsible for unleashing his destructive wrath, it is the sort of agreement that members of a dysfunctional family often accept. Anytime we do not behave spontaneously or speak truthfully because we will be blamed for upsetting someone who will hold us responsible for his (or her) anger, we are codependents.

BRUNNHILDE THE VALKYRIE: ARCHETYPAL FATHER'S DAUGHTER

We first meet an energetic, enthusiastic Brunnhilde, dressed in her shining armor, looking forward to going to a battle with her father Wotan. Wotan tells her that this is the day Siegmund will triumph with her help, and both father and daughter are in a heightened anticipatory mood. This pleasurable excitement is familiar to fathers' daughters, or "Daddy's little girls" of whatever age; they are about to do something together and enjoy the feeling that each is the other's "special buddy" or "special date."

Being a father's daughter such as Brunnhilde is at best a very affirming experience: she feels both competent like her father and attractive. However, if she becomes his primary attachment, closer to him than her mother, growing up and away from him becomes emotionally difficult if he is narcissistic and authoritarian. The first indication that there is a problem arises when there is a difference between them, when she does not react the way he anticipates or does not want to do what he wishes, and he either becomes angry or makes her feel guilty, or both.

Brunnhilde resembles the Greek goddess Athena, another father's daughter, who was known for her ability to think clearly and unemotionally. She was a warrior virgin goddess, usually portrayed wearing armor. Athena's mother was Metis, a goddess similar to Erda in being an earlier goddess of wisdom who had disappeared from sight. In Greek mythology, Athena is like a marble frieze that never changes: she stays forever virgin, forever her father's daughter, trusted by him to be of similar mind to him.

Athena is the archetypal pattern of the father's daughter, and if a woman identifies with this archetype, and her primary relationship is with a Zeus father or father figure, she does not develop further and her life is circumscribed by him. His will is identical with hers; what he thinks are her opinions; what he wants, she wants, too.

When Brunnhilde wants to refuse Wotan's command to abandon Siegmund, whom she has learned to love, and sorrowfully agrees to do so regardless of how she feels about it, she has momentarily decided that obedience to Wotan is more important than Siegmund's life. This is a moment of choice for Brunnhilde that is echoed in real life: when a parent demands that a significant relationship be broken off, will we obey, and at what cost?

SIEGMUND: OUTSIDER AND COMPASSIONATE HERO

Siegmund calls himself "Woeful," for woe has been his lot in life. His mother was murdered, his twin sister abducted, and his home burned to the ground. Homeless, he and his father then hunted together as Wolf and Wolfcub, until his father disappeared, leaving Siegmund to fend for himself, totally alone and unfamiliar with the ways of the world.

On trying "to make a friend or woo a maid," Siegmund has behaved inappropriately. Like a rustic who tries to fit into polite society and immediately reveals himself by his conversation and his ignorance about which fork to use, Siegmund blunders. However, the reason he has been "everywhere rejected" is not a matter of surface polish, though this was likely lacking. He perceives that he has deep differences in values that set him apart: "For what I thought was right, others reckoned was wrong, and what seemed to me bad, others held to be good."

As a recent example, we hear how Siegmund went to the rescue of a woman who was being forced by her brothers to marry a man whom she feared. When he did so and was attacked, it led to their deaths and hers. Siegmund was responding to her personal plight, which no one else considered important because it was immaterial; her brothers had the right to choose a husband for her and did not need to take her feelings into consideration. Siegmund, however, took her emotional distress to heart, and in doing so was wrong in a patriarchal context.

We also note Siegmund's sensitivity to the compromising position in which his presence may put Sieglinde. He is concerned not to bring misfortune to her by remaining there, even though it means his going back out into the storm.

Siegmund consistently acts from his feelings of compassion, passion, love, and loyalty. He assesses and responds to subjective feeling values that define what is good and bad or right and wrong and that matter to him far more than practical matters or political consequences. Acting from his heart rather than his head, he is consistent and consistently out of step, when what needs attending to in order to be acceptable or successful requires strategy, caring about property and property rights, observing rules, and taking who has power into consideration.

With the ardent tenderness and passion he feels for Sieglinde, who was forced against her will to marry Hunding, Siegmund claims her as his bride. That she is lawfully wedded to Hunding and as such is Hunding's possession, or that Sieglinde is his sister and there are prohibitions against brother-sister incest do not matter. Raised as Wolf-cub, he did not absorb societal attitudes and expectations, and he is instead guided purely by his feelings and instincts.

As an inner psychological situation, Siegmund and Sieglinde can represent the inner marriage of male and female halves as equals, with wholeness the potential. Their meeting and union can also represent the inner marriage of love and soul, eros and psyche, with joy the potential offspring of the union. It is this inner possibility of wholeness that makes us fall in love, as they did, "at first glance." We project onto the "beloved," our other half for whom we have been longing, the twin soul we have been seeking, or the lost part of ourselves we want to regain.

Siegmund as a symbolic figure is a man who acts from his heart, impulsively and without much thought about the situation, and he has had to pay the price. Compassion or love and passion for a woman motivate him. Described

THE VALKYRIE

in psychological terms, Siegmund is a man who above all is loyal to the feminine principle, which values love and relatedness more than law or power. In a world with patriarchal values, he is an outsider and outlaw in his disregard for law and convention.

As if to emphasize the feminine principle, which is often symbolized by the moon, Siegmund and Sieglinde see one another when the doors open suddenly, letting in the bright light of a full moon. In the moonlight, they gaze at features, recognize how they are related, and acknowledge and express the love they are feeling for one another. As contrasted to sunlight, which provides objective clarity and lends itself to seeing matters logically, moonlight illuminates subjective feelings in its softer glow.

SIEGLINDE, THE ABANDONED DAUGHTER AND DUTIFUL WIFE

Sieglinde's life has also been full of misfortune, with no choice until the moment Siegmund entered it. Abducted by the murderers of her mother and later forced against her will into marriage, she has had to accept that she is property and has become a dutiful wife. But once she feels the pull of love, it empowers her, and she takes the initiative, persuades Siegmund to stay, drugs her husband's drink, and comes to Siegmund in the night.

On the day of Sieglinde's marriage, an old man in gray with his hat covering one of his eyes appears. Though he looks at her with sorrow and solace, he does nothing to help her. By that glance, however, Sieglinde recognizes her father and realizes that he is abandoning her to this fate.

The young abandoned daughter symbolizes vulnerability, innocence, and budding feminine relationship values that are left behind by the ambitious man (or woman) who becomes intent on achieving power.

A daughter who is not valued or protected in a patriarchy is often abused. She has not learned to value herself, which makes her susceptible to becoming a victim. Also, a woman who is not under a man's protection is often thought of as "available" and may not have the strength to fend off unwanted attention.

SIEGLINDE AS A VICTIM: THE PSYCHOLOGY OF ABUSE

Sieglinde is tormented as she flees from Siegmund, whom she loves. The intimacy and rapture that she enjoyed in his embrace have turned into a frenzy of madness, and she is filled with shame. She flees from him in her attempt to get away from feelings of guilt and pain that followed their lovemaking. When Sieglinde's senses and soul respond sexually to Siegmund, floodgates of memory open.

Until Siegmund enters her house, Sieglinde has been benumbed and obedient, the dutiful wife of a man who has forced the marriage on her and with it his conjugal right to sex. This forced marriage came about after she had seen her mother murdered and her home pillaged and burned to the ground, and she had become the property of the very men who had done this. She probably was raped at the time. Memories of traumatic events are commonly repressed in childhood. They are too horrifying and overwhelming to think about, especially when there is no comfort or sanctuary available and further abuse is likely. Under such circumstances, memories and unexpressed emotions of grief, shame, horror, pain, and fear are buried alive in the psyche of victims. When they are evoked, even much later, we find that they can emerge as if the trauma just happened and can flood the person with affect. If this is too much for a fragile ego to bear, madness—loss of reality—can happen.

The psyche is protective, however, which is why childhood (or adult) traumas too terrible to remember are repressed. While these memories may surface in adulthood evoked by circumstances, as is happening to Sieglinde, what I see in my office is the return of memory only when there is a place of sanctuary and trust. Healing not madness results, but even within the safety of a therapeutic relationship, the intensity of the experience is such that the woman (or man) may fear that she is going mad. "I must be going crazy!" is commonly expressed, especially when the trauma occurred when the person was quite young. Sobbing wells up from the depths, racking the body; vivid images come back, there may be sensations in body parts of being violated. It can be so real that it intrudes upon ordinary reality with the force of an hallucination, as long dammed up emotional affect floods into consciousness bringing with it important fragments of the personality that had been lost from awareness.

Sieglinde has additional reasons to be in turmoil. When Sieglinde and Siegmund make love, it felt like a holy and sacred act, but it also brought back memories of sex with Hunding, which made her feel defiled, too dirty and guilty for "the purest of heroes." Whenever there is sexual abuse or forced sex, the child or woman suffers twice: first from what was done to her, and then from guilt because it happened.

As Sieglinde and Siegmund flee from Hunding, Sieglinde has terrible visions of dogs tearing at Siegmund. She sleeps fitfully, disturbed by her dreams, and we recognize by her words that she is reliving the time when her mother was murdered, her home was burned, and she was abducted: "Why doesn't father return? He is still in the woods. Mother! Mother! I feel afraid. Who are these strangers? Smoky darkness—smoldering fires—now they are flaring, flaming around—they burn the house—Oh, help me, brother! Siegmund! Siegmund!"

When memories of traumatic childhood events emerge, they do so vividly. Details and emotions come flooding back. Fear can be accompanied by guilty confusion when sexual abuse has taken place. There are repetitive nightmares, and the past can be confused with the present, especially when there is a perceived or misperceived present threat. Women who have been victims of trauma act like Sieglinde.

THE VALKYRIE

COMPASSION TRANSFORMS BRUNNHILDE

Siegmund reacts to Sieglinde's fear and flight with gentleness, promising to guard her from harm. She is asleep in his arms when Brunnhilde arrives to tell him that she has come for him. Following Wotan's orders, she is there to take him to Valhalla after he falls to Hunding in battle. She mistakenly assumes that Valhalla will be an attractive prospect for Siegmund. It is the ultimate reward for dying a hero: immortality in the company of other heroes, food and drink, and fair maidens who will wait on him.

Brunnhilde is astonished when Siegmund refuses to go if he must leave Sieglinde behind. When he hears of his imminent death, he grieves for the effect on Sieglinde. She is sleeping in his arms, trusting him to keep her from harm. Siegmund gazes upon Sieglinde and tells Brunnhilde that she offers him only "Valhalla's loveless pleasures." Shocked that he would reject Valhalla for this woman, she questions him and receives the brunt of his bitterness. Most important, she sees his distress and feels for him. His love and compassion for Sieglinde affect Brunnhilde greatly.

Siegmund is a man who truly, unnarcissistically loves, a man not interested in power or fame, one whose capacity for feeling and emotions is well developed, who knows that the shallowness of pleasure with beautiful women available to him because he is a hero cannot be compared to the depth of personal love and who intends to be loyal to the woman who trusts him.

When Siegmund hears that the sword he was given will shatter when he depends on it, he says, "Then shame on him who bestowed the sword." The contrast between Wotan, who turns his back on Siegmund, and Siegmund, who stands by Sieglinde, is markedly evident to us, as to Brunnhilde. When he learns that the sword will fail him later in battle, he draws it, addressing it as "this sword that a traitor bestowed on the true," and aims it at Sieglinde, who is still asleep, intending to take her life to spare her further suffering.

Brunnhilde is so moved that her obedience to Wotan dissolves. She is transformed into a compassionate woman who reacts in sympathy, putting feelings above duty to authority. Declaring that "the choice is mine!" she promises Siegmund that both he and Sieglinde will live, not knowing that Wotan himself will enter the battle to ensure Siegmund's defeat or the extent of Wotan's rage at her. Compassion has given her true courage—the capacity to act from the heart.

WOTAN AS AN EMOTIONALLY INCESTUOUS FATHER

In a dysfunctional family where there are anger and a lack of love between husband and wife, the relationship between a father and daughter often takes on an incestuous quality. As a child, the daughter may love her father unconditionally and think he is wonderful, while his wife sees his flaws and failures. As she grows older, the daughter who adores him gives him emotional support. She may become his confidante, the person who shares his thoughts. If he turns to her for companionship and validation, the daughter replaces his wife as his central relationship (and is thereby in an emotionally incestuous relationship with him). She mirrors back a positive image to him, in contrast to his wife, who may be critical and angry or the voice of reality that he does not want to hear.

Daughters idolize their fathers. For part or all of their lives he is their hero. He basks in the idealization, enjoying a mutual emotional love affair, and it usually hurts when a daughter adores or loves someone else as well. If he is psychologically healthy, though he does feel pangs of loss, he knows that she is growing up and becoming independent, as he would have her do. He also knows she loves him, knows that he has helped her to become a confident young woman and feels good about his father role.

However, if the father is both narcissistic and authoritarian, the daughter's independence is treated like a defection, and he defines her as rebellious and disobedient when she acts (or thinks) on her own. He responds with rage because he feels abandoned by her. There is an empty void at the center of a narcissistic personality, which is the reason the father needs power to control others; his rage helps protect him from the painful feelings of worthlessness and lack of love that originated in his own emotionally deprived childhood.

The shift in the father's behavior and attitude that the daughter's independence triggers is appalling to the child or young woman, who previously had basked in his good-will. Rage is an assault on the psyche; whether attacked verbally or physically, she is stunned. It is normal, healthy personality growth for a child or adolescent or adult to become an individual, different and separate from parents. However, Wotan is a needy and powerful narcissistic parent in an emotionally incestuous relationship with his daughter toward whom he is sexually attracted, which accounts for his reaction. Thus he behaves like a sexually jealous, spurned lover when Brunnhilde disobeys him. He imagines her laying with Siegmund, and the punishment he decrees is a sexual one: a stranger will find her unconscious and helpless, take her virginity, and become her master and husband (which can be interpreted as a projection of his own forbidden desire to possess her).

RAGE AS LOVE'S EXECUTIONER

Wotan's wrath at Brunnhilde's independence changes their relationship forever. In my psychiatric practice, I hear the truth of this—of the inhibition of a daughter's (or a son's) free and curious spirit, the repression of her spontaneity, and the blocking of feelings and thoughts that happen when a father (or mother) rages out of control, and the child learns fear. Then, like Brunnhilde, at Wotan's feet, raising her head timidly to speak softly to him, she becomes conciliatory and acutely sensitive to his moods.

Once the daughter has had the father's anger and power to punish directed at her, she knows that she must pay more attention to his feelings than to her own, which is the major lesson a codependent learns. In fact, she learns that having her own feelings and impulses puts her in danger of being attacked and accused of being rebellious, sexual, or selfish. Once a father rages out of control, it is a major traumatic event. He instills fear as the basis of behavior toward him and obedience as the required attitude. Love does not thrive under such circumstances and is replaced by fear.

Punitive rage is commonly used to keep men in line and to get them to obey without question, which is an essential requirement of the military. The marine drill instructor, for example, uses rage and humiliation deliberately to achieve this end, as do many football coaches. The military academies also do so, but in a more polished way. Fathers often use similar tactics to turn their boys into men. Whenever obedience to power is emphasized, feelings and thoughts that lead to independent behavior and compassion for others are systematically suppressed. Being loved and loving others have no place in power-based institutions (and a family can be one). Psychologically, when a man encounters an angry "Wotan" in his father, instructor, or boss, he gets lessons in how to behave. It leads him to devalue and then repress "Brunnhilde" and "Siegmund," the feminine and masculine caretaking and compassionate parts of himself.

THE MISSING MOTHER

Mother and maternal presence are notably absent in the *Ring of the Nibelung*. Among the immortals are Fricka,

who is a wife, not a mother, youthful Freya, the virgin warrior Valkyries, and Erda, who is a mother that her daughter
Brunnhilde never mentions. Siegmund and Sieglinde's
nameless mother was murdered. Sieglinde does have
maternal feelings for her unborn son, but as we will learn
in *Siegfried*, she dies in childbirth. There is a mother
deprivation in the *Ring of the Nibelung* (and other Western mythologies). A strong and loving mother is totally
absent from the lives of all of the characters in the *Ring*
cycle.

This is an accurate reflection of the desacralization of
feminine divinity in Western traditions and a corresponding devaluation and denigration of women. While some
mothers are both strong and loving, such mothers are
missing in patriarchal mythology and religions. The missing mother and maternal are a key to the dysfunctional
family dynamics and the emphasis on power in the *Ring of
the Nibelung*.

THE CONFLICTED FATHER

It is easy to characterize Wotan the god as an authoritarian
and narcissistic person, a model of a man whose need for
power and control dominates his personality and the people around him. Wotan, Zeus, and the sky gods of patriarchal religions and mythologies all are in this mold. They
personify patriarchal values. As an archetype, Wotan-Zeus
is the dominant one in men who seek and acquire power
over others.

However, there are other sides to Wotan's character, embodied as Wolf, Walse, and the Wanderer. As Walse, Wotan lived for a time as a human husband and father, and his children recall moments in which they felt his tender affection. As Wolf, he taught his young son how to survive in the wilds as a hunter or predator, leaving him to fend for himself when he was able to be on his own, promising him that when he needed a sword, he would be provided one. As the wanderer, Wotan was a solitary figure who asked questions, observed, and sought wisdom.

Siegmund recollects that when his father looked at him with affection, he thought of him as Walse, not Wolf. Walse was also the name that Sieglinde remembered calling their father, whom she recognized as the old man dressed in gray. Wotan abandoned his children in his quest for power. As Walse, he could genuinely love his children, which they felt. The children of ambitious men often have similar recollections, of times of love and closeness when he was present, and of feeling abandoned and forgotten, when their father got caught up in "being Wotan."

Wotan has a capacity for introspection and regret. When he tells Brunnhilde his thoughts, he speaks of how he acquired power and at what cost, and of his experience with love. He tells her that he has had his share of youthful pleasures and that when they waned, he "longed for might." Driven by this desire, he has been extraordinarily successful. As Wotan says, "I won myself the world."

The power over the world that he won is secured by treaties that are craftily made. He knows he acted wrongly to get power, and that seeds of evil are contained in the means that he used. Power does not bring him peace or security, and "the longing for love would not leave me."

Wotan has felt love as desire and pleasure and has taken risks for it. When he courted and won Fricka, he was willing to wager his good eye for her. Later, to Fricka's grief, he betrayed this love. He felt paternal love for Siegmund and Sieglinde and then abandoned them to suffer their fate. He loved his daughter Brunnhilde and then turned on her in rage.

While the conflict between power and love is the strongest theme in Wotan's psyche and in the *Ring of the Nibelung*, Wotan also sought wisdom. In *The Rhinegold*, Erda emerges out of the rocky ground high in the mountains to tell him to relinquish the ring and to predict the downfall of the gods. Wotan heeds her and gives up the ring. He recognizes the authority of wisdom and wants to know more. Wotan tells Brunnhilde of the impact Erda had on him: "When I asked her to say more, she vanished; in silence she sank from sight. Then I lost all my joy in life; my only desire was to learn."

Wotan seeks love and wisdom as well as power, but time and time again, power wins out and contaminates or subordinates the love or wisdom he feels or seeks.

Love and wisdom or power? These are soul choices we all face and make in the course of life as does Wotan. Choice by choice we decide, and each choice has an effect on who we are in the process of becoming, which is our inner story.

THE VALKYRIE

THE COURAGEOUS DAUGHTER AS HERO
AND ANIMA FIGURE

In the libretto of the *Ring of the Nibelung,* Brunnhilde is actually far different than the caricatured image we have of her. Her name conjures up pictures of middle-aged, buxom, Germanic sopranos wearing horned helmets. When we first meet Brunnhilde in *The Valkyrie,* she is a spirited, beautiful, young woman, the apple of her father's eye, a daughter who thinks as he does and thinks he is wonderful.

Then the feeling realm of Siegmund and Sieglinde enters into Brunnhilde's once circumscribed world. She has been an emotionally distant, invulnerable, virgin goddess. Through witnessing their love and pain, she becomes aware of human compassion, passion, devotion, loyalty, grief, madness, and self-sacrifice. She empathizes with Siegmund, is moved to be merciful, and decides against her father's command. Since he has warned her of the fury she will unleash if she disobeys him, this is an act of courage, though the cost of this disobedience will not become horrifyingly evident until later.

Wotan says that he wanted to create a "free hero" and despairs that all he can father are slaves. He fails to appreciate that Brunnhilde becomes a free hero, when she acts on her own with courage and decisiveness.

Every father's daughter has a potential "conflict with Wotan" unless she totally submerges any thoughts or feelings or choices of her own. The "conflict with Wotan" is an inner one as well, for she has to contend with her father's (or patriarchy's) expectations, opinions, and values that she has internalized. Individuation—the process of becoming an authentic person true to oneself and the process of growth toward the Self that makes life meaningful spiritually—requires that a man or woman dialogue with Wotan as a symbol of outer expectations and differentiate from him by rejecting fear and power as the ruling principles that motivate choice and action.

The Brunnhilde who goes against Wotan's will can also represent the growth of a man's feminine aspect, a symbol for his soul or anima. The anima in a man influences him to be faithful to whom he loves and loyal to those who love and depend upon him; she puts compassion ahead of abstract principles or obedience to authority. As an inner figure, "she" puts a man in conflict with his "Wotan."

The inner story in each of us contains Wotan and Brunnhilde somewhere. I find that myths help us to identify the voices within us and the tensions between them. On our own soul's journey, "who" we listen to matters. Wotan puts Brunnhilde to sleep. This is what happens in the inner lives of real people, if, in their obedience to authority or obsession with power, they are without compassion or mercy.

The Valkyrie tells us something about the struggle and suffering of the soul, and of how we evolve psychologically through experiences that change us. Like all of the characters in the *Ring*, we cannot control events or make people love us as we want to be loved. What we do when "this is how it is" is the challenge that life presents to us: whether we grow on a soul level through our choices or are diminished by what we do. "Who" we become as a result of our response to life is everyone's inner story.

SIEGFRIED *kills the dragon. Psychologically, a dragon fight is with something that is destructive to us. Even when the dragon seems to be a real person or an addiction, it is the susceptibility to be overcome that the hero in us must defeat.*

SIEGFRIED

THE HERO AS
AN ADULT CHILD

CAST OF CHARACTERS

Siegfried: *orphaned son of Siegmund and Sieglinde, who was raised in ignorance of his parentage by Mime*

Mime: *the dwarf and foster parent of Siegfried, brother of Alberich*

The Wanderer: *Wotan, the chief god, disguised as an old man who wears a broad-brimmed hat that covers his blind eye*

Alberich: *the dwarf who forged the ring of the Nibelung and is obsessed with getting it back*

Fafner: *the dragon who guards the hoard of the Nibelung, which includes the ring and the Tarnhelm; once a giant, he murdered his brother Fasolt to obtain the ring and transformed himself into the dragon with the Tarnhelm*

Erda: *goddess of wisdom who resides deep within the earth, mother of Brunnhilde*

Brunnhilde: *the Valkyrie, daughter of Wotan and Erde, whom Wotan punished for disobeying him*

The woodbird: *Siegfried's informant and guide*

CHAPTER 3

SIEGFRIED

The Hero as an Adult Child

The Story

SIEGFRIED IS THE MAIN CHARACTER IN THE THIRD OPERA IN
the cycle. Since the events in *The Valkyrie*, at least twenty
years have passed. Siegfried is an adult, the son of Siegmund
and Sieglinde. Siegmund was killed in battle by Hunding after
his sword Notung was shattered by Wotan's spear. Sieglinde was
rescued by Brunnhilde and fled into hiding. She died in childbirth, attended only by the dwarf Mime, who found her weep-
ing in the forest and brought her to his cave. (Mime is
Alberich's bullied brother from *The Rhinegold*.) Punished by
Wotan for disobedience, Brunnhilde has for all these years been
asleep on a mountain surrounded by fire.

SIEGFRIED AND MIME

Mime is alone in his cave, which is his forge and home. He has
made a large sword and is muttering to himself, complaining
that he works at making swords fit for a giant only to have "an
insolent Siegfried laugh and snap it in two as if I'd made him a

toy." Mime is dejected because he does not have the skill to forge the fragments of Notung together. Mime's ambition is to make a sword with which Siegfried can kill Fafner the dragon, so that "the Nibelung ring will come to me."

Preceded by the sound of his horn, Siegfried enters the cave, leading a large bear on a rope leash with the intention of frightening Mime. He succeeds. Mime runs behind the forge in fear, and Siegfried laughs at the sight. Our first impression of Siegfried is of a big bullying child in the body of a grown man, who takes pleasure in scaring Mime, whom he calls a "lazy smith." Siegfried wants him to make him a sword and says that he brought the bear to teach him to hurry. When Mime tells him that he just finished making one, Siegfried unties the bear, flicks him on the rump with the rope, and sends him loping off into the forest.

After the bear leaves, Siegfried sits down and recovers from his laughter, and Mime comes out from behind the forge to anxiously hand him the newly made sword, which Siegfried grabs from him. He looks at it and says scornfully, "A feeble pin! You call it a sword?" smashing it across the anvil. It splinters into pieces. Mime shrinks from his anger, terrified, as Siegfried rages at him, calling him an "ancient, doddering dwarf," saying that he should have broken it over Mime's head instead.

Mime remains out of his way and responds to this abuse by whining to Siegfried about his ingratitude, especially because Mime "loves him so much." Siegfried turns his back on him and refuses to listen. Ignored, Mime gets Siegfried some food and approaches him, saying, "Food is what you need. Come try this meat I have roasted, or would you prefer this soup? I fixed both just for you." Without even turning around, Siegfried strikes the bowl and meat out of Mime's hands. At this, Mime wails about everything he has done for Siegfried, how worn out he is, and how all he gets is scorn and hate.

Siegfried turns around to face Mime, to tell him that he cannot endure the sight of him because "I see that you are evil in

SIEGFRIED

all that you do." Siegfried roams the forest, trying to avoid him, yet he comes back. "What is it that makes me return? If you're so wise, tell me that," he asks.

Mime insists it is because Siegfried really loves him, that Mime is to Siegfried what "the mother birds are to fledglings," which prompts Siegfried to recall, "The birds were singing so sweetly in spring, their songs were loving and tender; and you replied when I asked you why that they were mothers and fathers. They chattered so fondly and were never apart. They built a nest and brooded inside, and soon little fledglings were fluttering there. The parents cared for the brood. And here in the woods, the deer lay in pairs, and savage foxes and wolves, too. Food was brought to the den by the father; the mother suckled the young ones. I learned from them what love must be. You must tell me, Mime, where your dear little wife is. Where is my mother, tell me?"

Mime denies that these examples apply to Siegfried: "I am your mother and father in one," he declares.

Siegfried tells Mime he lies: "Every young one is like his parents. I know because I've seen it myself." One day, he reports, he saw his own reflection in a stream. "I saw my face, and it wasn't like yours, not in the least—no more than a toad resembles a fish. No fish had a toad for a father!" Mime responds that this comparison is stupid and absurd.

Siegfried has been searching for the truth and has come to many conclusions, including the reason that he returns: to find the truth of his parentage, which only Mime can tell him. When reasoning and argument do not work, Siegfried seizes Mime by the throat, saying, "I must force you to tell me! All kindness is wasted on you. You'll only answer if I strike you."

With his hands choking Mime, Siegfried demands to know, "Who are my father and mother?" The truth emerges in pieces. Mime is self-pitying and self-serving as Siegfried presses him for details, which Mime begrudgingly supplies. He tells Siegfried that his mother Sieglinde died in childbirth and gave Siegfried his name. Mime maintains, however, that he does not know the name of Siegfried's father, only that he died in battle. When Siegfried demands to see some proof if he is to trust the story, Mime brings him the pieces of his father's fragmented sword, Notung.

Siegfried orders Mime to forge them together this very day, and then he leaves. Siegfried does not know that Mime is not up to the task; otherwise, he would have done it long ago. Furthermore, Mime is in a bind. He cannot make the only sword that can kill the dragon who possesses the ring of the Nibelung; and now, even if he could forge this sword, Siegfried would take it and leave. How is he to get the ring of power that he covets when he needs Siegfried and Notung to accomplish the task for him?

WOTAN THE WANDERER AND MIME

Mime is at his smithy, slumped over and dejected, when an old man enters wearing a long cloak and a broad-brimmed hat that hangs down over one eye and carrying a spear that he uses as a staff. It is Wotan, in his disguise of "the Wanderer." Though Mime wants to have nothing to do with him, Wotan engages Mime in conversation, betting his head that he can answer any three questions. Mime wastes this opportunity by asking him questions whose answers he already knows. One answer is psychologically revealing: asked who rules the heights, the Wanderer replies, "Light-Alberich, Wotan," thereby acknowledging similarities between himself and Alberich.

After answering Mime's questions, Wotan reminds him that the law demands that Mime now reciprocate and place his head on the line. When Wotan takes his turn, he asks about Siegfried's parentage and the name of his father's sword, information that Mime provides. Then he asks the one question that Mime himself wants to know: "Whose hand can make new these fragments—who will forge Notung?"

Wotan provides the answer as a riddle: "One who has never learned to fear."

SIEGFRIED FORGES HIS SWORD

Siegfried comes back, expecting that Mime by then will have forged his sword, to find him cowering under the anvil. Mime had imagined Fafner the dragon coming after him. Siegfried laughs at him and pokes fun at the sight. "What are you doing there? Were you sharpening my sword?"

Mime comes out from hiding, saying, "The sword? The sword? How can I forge it? It can be done only by one who has never learned to fear—how could I do such work?"

These thoughts lead Mime to ponder aloud how he failed to teach Siegfried fear. He manages to persuade Siegfried that fear is something he needs to learn. To Siegfried, the concept is so foreign that he asks, "Is it a skill, a craft? Speak and teach me what fear is!" Mime tells him it is easily learned. Fafner can teach him.

When Mime confesses that he cannot remake Notung, Siegfried tells him to give him the fragments, that he will forge his father's sword himself. He then builds a hotter fire in the forge and begins to file the fragments into splinters. Mime tells him he is doing it all wrong, that he should use the hot solder. However, Siegfried continues to shred the fragments, saying that there will be "no patched sword" for him. He works the bellows, increasing the heat, melts down the splinters, pours the molten steel into a mold, plunges the mold into water, takes it out of the mold, and hammers and shapes it on the anvil. All the while, he sings about Notung as the sword of his need— recalling to us that this is how his father Siegmund once saw it.

In the meantime, Mime is thinking furiously. He sees that the sword is being forged and anticipates that Fafner will be killed, "and the gold and the ring passed to the boy." By wit and guile, he is determined to get the ring for himself, and he comes up with a murderous plot. Mime figures that Siegfried will be thirsty after the fight. Mime will give him a sleeping potion in the drink to quench his thirst, and when he is asleep, Mime will seize the sword and "simply chop off his head"; then the ring and the gold will be his.

SIEGFRIED KILLS THE DRAGON

Outside of Fafner's lair, deep in the forest, in the dark of night, Alberich and Wotan meet. Alberich lurks here because the ring he forged and covets is inside guarded by Fafner. The ring also draws Wotan (as the Wanderer) here. Wotan wants it for himself, but the possibility that Alberich might someday regain it obsesses him as well. Like Mime, Alberich lacks the power to kill the dragon himself, while Wotan is constrained from doing so by the agreement he made with Fafner and Fasolt. Alberich reminds him that if he did, the spear with which he rules, upon which the agreement is engraved, would "snap like a straw." Alberich, Mime, and Wotan each need someone else to kill the dragon in order to get their hands on the ring.

Wotan tells Alberich that Mime is on the way to Fafner's cave, leading Siegfried, who will kill the dragon. He warns Alberich to beware of Mime and then leaves. Alberich hides himself in a cleft in the cliff to watch and wait.

As day breaks, Mime and Siegfried arrive. Siegfried accompanies Mime to Fafner's lair in order to learn fear. Mime now itemizes what there is about Fafner to be afraid of: he tells Siegfried how huge Fafner is, that he could eat him in a single gulp, that poisonous foam pours from his mouth, that his scaly tail lashes around, and that if he catches Siegfried in his coils he will crush all his bones. These dangers do not scare Siegfried in the least. His only concerns are: "Does Fafner have a heart?" and "Is it located in the usual place?" On being assured that

S I E G F R I E D

Fafner does and it is, Siegfried tells Mime that he will kill Fafner. In the meantime, he orders Mime to get out of his sight.
Mime leaves, wishing to himself that Fafner and Siegfried
would kill each other.

Siegfried stretches out under a tree and delights in being alone
in the woods. Of Mime, he says to himself, "So he's no father of
mine; that thought fills my heart with joy!" He listens to the mur-
muring sounds of the forest and falls into a reverie, wondering
about his father and mother. He concludes that his father must
have looked like him, but he cannot even imagine his mother.
"How this son longs to see his mother!" he says to himself.

As he lies under the tree in thought, Siegfried notices that
the sounds of birds are becoming louder and more beautiful. It
makes him wish that he could understand what they were saying, which inspires him to cut a reed to see if he can mimic the
song. When his attempts are unsuccessful, he decides to play
the birds a tune on his horn, pausing after each long sustained
note to see if there is a response. The horn arouses Fafner, who
emerges from his lair and makes a noise like a loud yawn.

Siegfried is astonished at the sight of the huge, scaly dragon,
but he is unafraid. Fafner notices Siegfried, and asks, "Who is
there?" That the great beast speaks is a surprise. Siegfried
inquires if he is prepared to teach him what fear is. Fafner
would rather eat him than have a conversation, and so he
comes at Siegfried with breakfast in mind. Siegfried draws his
sword, avoids Fafner's lashing tail and his poisonous venom,
and wounds him. At this, the dragon roars and rears up, expos-
ing his breast, allowing Siegfried to thrust Notung deep into his
heart, inflicting a mortal wound. The dying dragon tells Siegfried, "Fafner, the last of the giants, falls at the hands of a boy!"

As Siegfried withdraws his sword from the dead dragon,
some of the dragon's blood gets on his hand, which burns.
When he raises his hand to his mouth to cool it, he tastes the
blood and immediately is able to understand the language of
the birds. The woodbird is singing to him. She tells him of the

Nibelung hoard lying in the cave, of the Tarnhelm, whose magic will serve him, and of the ring, which will make him lord of the world. Siegfried thanks the bird for this information and disappears into Fafner's cave to claim the treasure.

Once Siegfried is out of sight, Mime stealthily returns. He checks to make sure that Fafner is dead and then cautiously moves toward the cave. At this point, Alberich emerges from the rocks and rushes forward to block Mime's way. The two call each other names and fight over which one will get the ring. Mime says he deserves it as pay for the years he slaved bringing Siegfried up. Alberich's scorn at this is intimidating; he will not even consider sharing the treasure with Mime. He will take it all; there will be nothing for Mime: "Not a trinket, not a nail-head." This sends Mime into a rage, and he threatens Alberich that he will set Siegfried against him. "Better turn around," Alberich suggests, for he sees Siegfried coming, and, much to their distress, he is carrying the Tarnhelm and the ring.

Siegfried looks at his prizes thoughtfully, not knowing how to use them. To him, they are only pretty trophies, proof that he killed a dragon. With this in mind, he puts the ring on his finger and hangs the Tarnhelm from his belt. Now the wood-bird begins singing once more. She warns him to beware of the treacherous dwarf and tells him that if he listens carefully when Mime speaks, the dragon blood will allow him to understand what Mime really means; he has been "made wise" by the taste of Fafner's blood.

Mime comes creeping in unobtrusively. He watches Siegfried and decides that he will be doubly sly and use his friendliest flattery. He comes closer to Siegfried, and they begin a dialogue. Musically, Mime sings affectionately and tenderly, but each time Siegfried hears the truth: that he was "never hard to deceive," that Mime has hated him and his kind, and that "love played no part in bringing you up."

SIEGFRIED

Mime's voice is affectionate, his intent deadly. Mime is trying to persuade Siegfried to accept a drink from him, one drop of which will put Siegfried to sleep and allow Mime to steal the ring and the Tarnhelm. After this he will chop off Siegfried's head. When Mime pours his poisoned brew into a drinking horn and offers it to Siegfried, Siegfried raises his sword and strikes Mime dead.

Siegfried drags Mime's body to Fafner's cave and throws it inside. Then, with great effort, he blocks the mouth of the cave with the dragon's body. He is hot from this exertion and seeks the protective shade of the tree. He lies underneath it and gazes up at the branches, where he sees the woodbird again: "You're back then, dearest woodbird; you've not flown away after the fight?" Above him, he sees his woodbird and her brothers and sisters chirping and swaying, surrounding her with laughter and love. He compares his sad plight with theirs: he is alone, without brothers or sisters; he never knew his parents, and now he has killed "a detestable dwarf," who was, however, his only companion.

"Dear little woodbird, can you be my guide? Can you tell me where I'll find a friend?" he asks of the bird who has advised him so well. From above, he hears the voice of the woodbird telling him that now that he is free from the evil dwarf, he "must awake his glorious bride: high on a mountain she sleeps, guarded by threatening flames." Siegfried learns that whoever awakens the maiden Brunnhilde has her for his bride, and that whoever can cross through the flames "must be unacquainted with fear."

Hearing this, he thinks aloud, "A foolish boy, unacquainted with fear? Dear woodbird, why, that's me!" The woodbird now flutters in a circle above him and hesitantly flies off. Siegfried, realizing that she wants him to follow her, exclaims, "You guide me; where you flutter, there I shall go!"

WOTAN AND ERDA

The scene shifts. It is a stormy night, and the sky is full of lightning and thunder. Wotan, in his guise of the Wanderer, has come to summon Erda out of the earth and deep sleep. She appears as a mysterious figure glowing with a bluish light, wondering who is disturbing her and why. In her sleep she dreams; in her dreams she broods; from her brooding all her wisdom comes. While she sleeps, the three Norns are awake, weaving all she knows into their cord.

Wotan wakes her seeking wisdom and counsel. Why not consult the Norns instead; they weave "all that I know," she responds. "They spin what you tell them but cannot change that world with their weaving," Wotan replies. He wants to know how he can stop "the swiftly turning wheel," if events that he set in motion can be brought to a halt.

Erda tells him that her wisdom has been clouded since he conquered her. He should ask Brunnhilde instead. "She is valiant and wise as well, so why wake me? You will learn your answer from our child." When he explains that he cannot do this because Brunnhilde lies asleep on a rock as punishment for disobeying him, and that pride was the cause of her defiance, Erda is silent for a long time. When she does speak, her questions are penetrating and confronting: "How can pride's teacher punish pride? How can he who urged the doing, punish the deed? How can he who rules by right, to whom truth is sacred, scorn what is right and rule by falsehood?"

Erda wants to go back to sleep, but Wotan prevents her from doing so. He blames her for his "fear of ruin and shameful downfall," which he attributes to her words of warning and doom. He wants her to tell him how to master his anxieties, to tell him "how a god can master his care."

Erda neither accepts Wotan's blame nor tells him how to manage. Instead, she tells him that he is not what he claims to be. He retorts that she is not the wise dreamer she once was,

SIEGFRIED

either. Both evaluations are accurate. The gods are not what they once were; their time is passing. Earlier, Wotan anguished over ever losing his power over the world and was bitter at the prospect. Now he tells Erda that he bequeaths it to Siegfried, who has the ring, and to Brunnhilde, whom Siegfried will awaken with a kiss. Erda can return to endless sleep and dream of the gods' destruction, for he will gladly yield his rule to the young.

SIEGFRIED MEETS WOTAN

Erda has disappeared, and Wotan the Wanderer is alone, when Siegfried comes upon him. The woodbird that led him this far, saw Wotan, became alarmed, and flew off. Siegfried is determined that he will continue on "the path my bird pointed out," but now he will have to discover it on his own. Wotan sees him looking around and asks, "Young man, where are you going?"

Siegfried tells Wotan that he seeks a sleeping maiden on a mountain surrounded by fire. Wotan wants to know who told him to do this. In the conversation that follows, Siegfried tells Wotan how he killed the dragon, whose blood made him able to understand the woodbird.

When Wotan asks, "But who made the fragments from which you forged the sword?" Siegfried replies, "Ha! How can I tell? I only know that the broken sword was useless until I forged it myself." His response amuses and pleases Wotan, who laughs with good humor. Siegfried feels mocked, however, and tells him, "Old man, if you can help me, then do so. If you can't, hold your tongue!" Wotan retorts, "Young man, be patient! If I seem old, then you should honor the aged."

"Honor the aged!" Siegfried exclaims. He had enough of elderly Mime, of whom he is now rid, and now another old man is standing in his way. "If you obstruct me, you'll suffer Mime's fate," he threatens. Siegfried takes a step closer to Wotan, which

RING OF POWER

is an intimidating gesture, insolently comments on how strange he looks, and wants to know why he wears such a huge hat. When he notices that it covers a missing eye, he says, "Doubtless someone put it out when you barred his way. Make yourself scarce, or else you may lose the other eye, too."

Wotan warns Siegfried to be careful, that he is as blind as the eye that Wotan has lost. Siegfried laughs rudely and is impatient with him. He calls Wotan "a foolish old man" and demands that he show him the path, saying, "Speak, or I'll push you aside."

"If you knew who I am, you'd spare me your scorn," Wotan replies. He hints at who he is and warns Siegfried not to awaken his rage, for it would ruin them both. All of this goes over Siegfried's head; Wotan is just a chattering old man who still has not replied to his question, as far as he is concerned. And Siegfried is a brash, insensitive young man without manners or respect in his treatment of Wotan.

Siegfried tells Wotan, "Out of my way, stubborn old fool!" as he decides to find the path to the slumbering maid on his own.

Wotan has had enough of being conciliatory, and reaping insolence in return. He is angry. He tells Siegfried that the woodbird left him to save its life, for it recognized him as the ruler of ravens. Asserting his authority, Wotan tells Siegfried, "You shall not tread any further on the path that it showed you!"

Siegfried is astonished and unintimidated, "Ho! Ho! So you'd stop me! Who are you to say I can't go on?!" he asks defiantly. Wotan tells Siegfried that it was he who cast the spell around the sleeping maid and surrounded her with a sea of fire. He further informs Siegfried that the man who can walk through the fire, wake her, and win her "makes me powerless forever!" To bar Siegfried's way and demonstrate his power, Wotan points his spear at the mountains high above: at this gesture from him, the fire rages up, lightning flashes, and clouds of fire roll toward them, moving like a flash flood of fire.

SIEGFRIED

Instead of backing off, as Wotan assumes he will, Siegfried, who is unafraid of fire, advances. The fire shows him where Brunnhilde is; Wotan has shown him the way to her after all. The billowing flames do not bother Siegfried, nor do they teach him respect for Wotan's power.

Wotan, who is not gladly yielding his rule to the young, as he told Erda he would, now bars Siegfried's way with his spear. "The sword that you carry was broken by this shaft, and once again I'll break it on this spear!" Wotan asserts.

Hearing this, Siegfried draws his sword, saying, "Then my father's foe faces me here? Sweet is the vengeance that has come my way. Swing your spear and see it break on my sword!" With one blow, Siegfried strikes the spear in two. Lightning and thunder split the air and die away. A subdued Wotan picks up the pieces, tells Siegfried, "Pass on, I cannot prevent you!" and disappears into the darkness.

Siegfried's attention is drawn to the clouds of fire that have rolled down the mountain. Unafraid, he welcomes them as the pathway to Brunnhilde. Raising his horn, he plays his call, then plunges into the flames to find and wake her.

SIEGFRIED AWAKENS BRUNNHILDE

Siegfried has been climbing the cliff and has just reached the summit. He looks around with wonder. First he notices a magical horse in deep sleep near some pine trees at the edge of the clearing; then he is drawn by the flash of sunlight on gleaming armor, to a sleeping figure, covered by a large shield. He removes it and sees Brunnhilde, her head in a helmet, her body in armor. He assumes that he is looking at a man but finds that his "heart is strangely stirred." Carefully, he loosens the helmet and takes it off. Brunnhilde's fair, long curling hair falls down and frames her sleeping face.

RING OF POWER

Siegfried, still thinking that this is a man, removes the armor, cutting through the rings of mail to remove the breast-plate. Then he lifts it off and sees the shapely body of Brunn-hilde, the first woman he has ever gazed upon, which has an astonishing effect on him. He feels under an enchantment; there is a burning feeling in his chest; his heart grows feeble and faint. He calls, "Mother, Mother, help me!"

Brunnhilde's sleeping form arouses Siegfried; he feels anguish and yearning. He falls upon her breast, looks at her, gets up, wonders if this is what fear is, calls upon his mother again, and finally decides he will kiss her.

Brunnhilde is awakened by Siegfried's kiss; slowly she sits up and gazes around her. She hails the sunlight and the sky, which she is seeing for the first time after her long sleep, before she asks, "Who is this man who wakes me to life?"

Siegfried is deeply moved and tells her that it is he who has awakened her. The two of them ecstatically sing of the joy and blessing they feel as they look upon each other's radiance, each basking in the enraptured gaze of the other. When Brunnhilde tells Siegfried that she has always loved him and that she sheltered him in Sieglinde's womb, he momentarily thinks that she really is his mother. Brunnhilde tenderly calls him an innocent child and tells him that he will never look upon his mother, "but we are one, if you can grant me your love." Siegfried is confused by her words and afraid of his yearning for her.

While Brunnhilde knows who Siegfried is and what has led up to this moment, Siegfried knows nothing of her. She points to her sacred horse, Grane, who awoke out of his enchanted sleep when she did, and speaks of her weapons and armor with which she sheltered heroes. As she is recalling the past with sadness, his ardor is growing. He realizes from what he has been told that since he awakened her she is his bride.

Now it is Brunnhilde's turn to be afraid. She is without her armor and is horrified at what losing her maidenhood will mean: she will be "dealt a wound" and no longer be Brunnhilde.

She wants Siegfried to stay away, to not come near her with passionate fury. She reminds him that he once saw his reflection in the shining stream and now sees himself reflected in her, but "when that water is stirred by a wave, that smiling reflection will break and be gone." Telling him to love himself and leave her in peace, she pleads, "Do not destroy this maid who is yours!"

"Burning, I long for those cooling waters," is Siegfried's response. He tells Brunnhilde he wants to "leap in the stream—if only those waves could engulf me forever." He becomes eloquent in his passion and embraces her. She responds, "A fire is kindled; can you not feel it?" In the mutuality of this momentary enchantment, Siegfried's fear fades, and Brunnhilde joyfully prophesies what their union will bring: Valhalla will fall to dust, the era of the gods will end, the rope of destiny will be severed, and she will live by the light of Siegfried's bright star. He will be her joy, her wealth, her world. He in turn tells her how she is his joy, his wealth, his world, his all. They are exultant. As they pledge their love, each ends with the words: "Light of our loving, laughter in death!"

The Hero as an Adult Child

MIME BEHAVES LIKE A MARTYR-MOTHER TO SIEGFRIED, who acts the part of an ungrateful adult-child. Mime sees himself as a long-suffering, devoted, and unselfish parent, who does everything for Siegfried, while Siegfried is hostile to Mime and avoids him as much as he can. Mime's words and attitude are those of a guilt-inducing, depressed, angry, and resentful parent.

Such a parent is usually the mother, with a psychology similar to Mime's. Like him, she feels that she has no direct power and cannot gain respect from others or have a position in the world on her own. She may resent a brother or a husband who bullied her (as Alberich abused Mime) and had opportunities that she did not have, even though her intelligence or talents were equal to or greater than his. In patriarchal families where boys are favored and educated, injustice and inequality are the norms as they are in dysfunctional families where emotional incest makes one child the favorite, or scapegoating makes another child victimizable by everyone else.

When children are openly treated unequally or unfairly because of favoritism or discrimination, objections or anger at the injustice usually are punished, and aspirations to rise above an assigned inferior role are ridiculed or discounted. Such children in abusive families learn to be ingratiating, manipulative, indirect, and patient so as not to provoke anger. It is adaptive to do so, as women, minorities, poor people, incarcerated men, and men in the lower rungs of hierarchical situations know. How much freedom of expression a person has has to do with where he or she is in the pecking order or ladder and the character and capacity to love of those with greater power. Thoughts and feelings that if expressed would provoke anger or punishment are often put out of awareness.

As a result, a devalued woman or man becomes psychologically deformed. Healthy aspirations for power to express and actualize herself become stunted, and she

S I E G F R I E D

lacks self-esteem and confidence. Her animus—or inner male—which Jung defines as the more traditionally masculine aspects of the personality to do with will, competitiveness, assertion, aggressiveness, and logical thinking—becomes dwarfed; metaphorically her animus comes to look like Mime.

THE DEVOURING MOTHER

When a woman's ability to achieve anything for herself has been stunted and her marriage is dysfunctional, she may project her unlived aspirations upon her son: he will be her hero, who is to become the successful doctor, businessman, author, artist, whatever, who achieves status for her and lives out her unlived life. She may also look to him to fulfill her emotional needs for companionship, validation, and affection. Her projections, needs, and expectations can devour her son's individuality, making it difficult, sometimes even impossible, for him to know what he wants for himself or even to know what is authentically himself. He can take on responsibility for her happiness, attuning himself to her needs. When this happens to him, she becomes the archetypal devouring mother, who "incorporates" him; he becomes an extension of her, molded to meet her needs and expectations of him.

A fearsome hungry bear, with gaping jaws filled with sharp teeth, can be a symbol for the terrible devouring mother (or father). Mime is terrified when Siegfried brings a large bear into the cave, even though it is leashed.

Dreams of devouring animals or dangerous spiders come to both the person who is doing the "devouring," by being intrusively needy and entangling the other in a web of need and guilt, and the person who is being gobbled up in the relationship—and for good reason. The person who acts the part of the devouring mother has become "possessed" by this archetype, which takes her over and in so doing "devours" other aspects of herself as well. The casualties within her may include her observing ego, the good mother who wants what is truly best for her child and knows that independence from her is what he needs, as well as parts of herself unrelated to her maternal role. When a person becomes so identified with the needy, martyred mother that this is all she is, then everything in her that makes her a unique individual is devoured, at least temporarily.

When a woman is taken over by this archetype, her words, expressions, and actions become practically indistinguishable from those of countless other devouring mothers, or from Mime. Anyone who is susceptible to this should be terrified.

SIEGFRIED'S THREE TASKS

The bear comes growling at Siegfried when he sounds his horn throughout the forest. Siegfried, with his fearlessness and strength, puts a rope around the bear's neck, befriends it, and brings it home. It is a symbolic act, whose meaning is based upon what the bear represents to Siegfried. It is a male bear, feared for its aggressive strength and potential for ferocity. With his own brute strength and anger, Siegfried can also become destructive and ferocious. He and other physically strong men need to befriend and leash their aggressiveness and be able to summon and dismiss it, so that they and others do not need to fear this in themselves.

Siegfried wants a strong sword and looks to Mime to make him one. Mime's efforts are ineffectual. The swords he makes shatter. A good sword is finely honed yet strong; it endures and strikes blows without shattering or losing its edge. It cuts through matter. Traditionally, a man who carries a sword is a knight or warrior, trained and disciplined in his aggression. On a symbolic level, when a man acquires a sword, he acquires attributes of manhood. He can attack and can defend himself and others. The sharpness of the blade correlates with the ability to discriminate, to penetrate, to cut ties and losses, to be decisive and incisive in his thinking and action.

Cringing Mime cannot provide Siegfried with a sword any more than he can be a model for manhood. When Siegfried shatters the last of the series of swords Mime has made, he gives up the unrealistic expectation that Mime can give him the sword he needs. Only then does Siegfried get what he needs to make a sword himself. Giving up on unrealistic expectations of inadequate parents is a major task of growing up and a major task of psychotherapy. We are "adult children" until we face the truth of our parents' inadequacies and stop trying to get what we want or need from parents who cannot be more or do more than they are.

When Siegfried next turns his back on Mime and rejects the food he offers, Siegfried is rude, insolent, and abusive. Parental figures like Mime create sons (and sometimes daughters) who act like Siegfried. A doted upon and deferred to son, who hears insincerity, is manipulated, and finds that he is feared, is likely to become an insolent, rejecting "Siegfried," who can be described in today's terms as "a badly behaved adult child."

On a symbolic level, however, he, and anyone raised by a "Mime" actually needs to reject what the food he is offered represents: it is love that creates dependency or binds one with guilt, food or drink that numbs one to the reality of the situation, and words of affection that one must respond to as if genuine and reciprocated, regardless of how one really feels. However, even when parental nourishment is freely given and good for growth, as are unconditional love and affirmation, a time comes to leave home and seek sources of nourishment and growth in the world. In leaving home and growing up, the individual faces outward and moves away.

Siegfried comes home with a leashed bear, forges his own sword after he gives up the expectation that Mime will provide him one, and then refuses Mime's food. Once he completes these three acts, it means that he has symbolically gotten control of a destructive potential in himself; that he has freed himself from hoping that he can get something he needs and can never get from an inadequate parent (or parent substitute) and instead discovers it in himself; and that he turns away from his dependency on a parent (or parent substitute). These three tasks are metaphorically what adult children need to do in order to become adults. They also are the psychological tasks that mature adults have accomplished.

With "good enough" parents, this is achieved relatively easily compared to the difficulties and impediments that come from growing up in a dysfunctional family. A parent who is not in control of his or her "powerful and ferocious bear" lashes out with destructive words and/or physical abuse. Whether the child witnesses it directed at another family member or has it directed at himself or herself, that child is scarred and damaged as a result and often has difficulty with control of his or her own destructive impulses. Being in a household where anger and fear are in the air and people are unsafe makes these impulses stronger. "Leashing" is more difficult than in a family where clear communication and caretaking take place because of the intensity of hostile feelings generated in abusive dysfunctional families and because of the example set by parents. Out of this comes the likelihood that an abused child will become an abusive parent.

When a person is aware of his or her own power and has it under control (as Siegfried's leashing the bear can be interpreted to mean), when he is not afraid that the other person can inflict serious damage upon him, when he can take care of himself, then it is time to bring up unaddressed, difficult issues; only then is it possible to confront someone such as Mime, who has been withholding information and has (until then) the upper hand. This

RING OF POWER

Siegfried does, receiving pieces of information about his history, "the family secret," and pieces of his father's broken sword. Then he can forge an identity and a new sword of his own.

SIEGFRIED THE HERO WITHOUT FEELINGS

Siegfried is raised by Mime, who himself was abused, exploited, and unloved. As a consequence, Mime does not know how to love. He tries to teach Siegfried to love him, without loving Siegfried, which fails. He also tries to make Siegfried feel guilty, which also fails.

While he has not learned to feel, Siegfried has developed his ability to think logically. He arrives at conclusions drawn from reasoning. He finds discrepancies between what Mime has told him and his observations, and, armed with the logic of his thinking, he is able to confront Mime. This is his first intellectual combat. He prepares for it by honing his thoughts, which he articulates and delivers. He deftly parries Mime's lies, finds weak points in his story, presses his advantage, and uses force deliberately to extract the information and the pieces of the sword, thereby showing his mastery of a mental sword.

Siegfried observes birds and animals and arrives at some correct conclusions about feelings, but he has none of his own. He cannot feel either love or fear, two of the most basic emotions, without which he cannot have empathy or compassion, because he cannot imagine what another person might feel or be going through emotion-

SIEGFRIED

ally. It is impossible to make him feel guilty or remorseful, because for this he also has to be able to feel. He laughs at Mime for being afraid. It amuses him.

Without love and fear, it takes no courage to perform a heroic act. Siegfried thinks nothing of facing the dragon Fafner because he has no fear. It does not occur to him that he is at risk, for he is unaware of the possibility of vulnerability. He has no imagination about such things. Mime, in comparison, is fear ridden; his vivid imagination terrorizes him; he imagines Fafner, cringes and hides under the anvil.

Siegfried has been brought up in the forest, raised as much if not more by nature around him as by Mime. He has never even seen a woman and never had anyone to envy. If he were obsessed with acquiring anything, with his strength and sword, and lack of feelings, he could take it with no remorse for suffering it might cause others; he could be a psychopath. As is, he is an insensitive, uneducated, unsocialized young man who knows nothing about the world of relationships.

Like Alice Miller's subjects in *The Drama of the Gifted Child*, a book that focuses upon narcissistic mothers and their intelligent sons, Siegfried has been raised by a needy, self-centered parental figure who never was concerned about his feelings and needs. When a bright child depends upon a caretaker who habitually withholds from or punishes him when he does or says things that arise from his authentic feelings, he surmises that he must hide them and does, often suppressing them so well that he grows to adulthood not knowing what his feelings are.

In any family where appearances and productivity are the values, emotions and the ability to feel are not given much attention at best and are often suppressed. If the innate tilt—a person's psychological typology—is toward thinking rather than feeling, the realm of feelings remains undeveloped. This tendency is further compounded by expectations placed on males in a competitive society where success is the measure of the man. In the military, politics, and business, being tenderhearted is a handicap, and empathy is thus something to hide. The line between hero and psychopath becomes blurred in places. To be either depends upon what one does or is willing to do and on how much heartlessness or bending or breaking of the law, lack of concern for the consequences to others, and lack of concern for or risk to one's self a person will take.

LIBERATION FROM A NEGATIVE IDENTITY

Siegfried's joy at finding out that Mime is not his real father can be understood by anyone from a dysfunctional family who has felt contempt or shame toward a parent, especially if he or she has had the common fantasy that some children have in such circumstances. They feel that "these people are not my parents. This is not my family. I don't belong here." This fantasy or belief is present in many children who as adults do not become like their parents, or like their siblings whose lives are a direct continuation of the dysfunctional family story, carried into the next generation. As children, these survivors were able to get away from a harsh or unfeeling reality by retreating inward. Reading and their imagination helped them to believe that they would someday find people who will be their "real family." Their quest for people who are kind, intelligent, or successful propels them out into the world to find friends, surrogate families, and mentors.

Siegfried's joy at knowing that Mime is not related to him is also analogous to the experience of becoming free of a negative identification. People grow up accepting that they are what others said they were when they were children. In psychotherapy or life, a time may come when they realize that this is not so: they are not stupid, or unattractive, or whatever negative belief they had accepted as true about themselves. Like Siegfried, who realizes that he is not related to Mime, there is joy at discovering that one is not "a Nibelung."

Siegfried also finally hears the truth, which validates his own experience. He grew up hearing Mime tell him how much he loved him, how much he has sacrificed and suffered and cared for him, and Siegfried never felt it. To finally have Mime tell him that he has hated him all along is liberating. There is a joy at knowing you have not been ungrateful and unloving toward someone who has genuinely loved you. It is a relief to finally learn that your mistrust or suspicion was based on reality. When there is a discrepancy between what a significant person says in words and what is conveyed nonverbally by his or her facial expression, voice, and actions or picked up by intuition, it is confusing at the very least and can literally be crazy making, at worst.

Liberation from a negative identity, finding the truth, or becoming free of the enmeshment in whatever the particular negative family dynamics are usually brings both joy and sorrow. Siegfried, in reverie under the tree, moves from joy to longing for the mother love he has never had. A child in a dysfunctional family often is lonely, but he or she often becomes lonelier still when separating from them in adulthood. To become free, a person must be able to tolerate separateness, which is always aided by meditation, by the ability to tune in to inner thoughts, feelings, sensations, or intuitions and to reflect upon them. Only then does one begin to hear an inner voice that can become a good counselor. This is metaphorically what is happening to Siegfried as he listens to the sounds of the forest.

Most mythological heroes grow up without a father, or without knowing that their true father is a hero or god. A son who can follow his father's footsteps usually does. When this is impossible for him to do because he rejects his father, was rejected by him, or has no father, then he has to find his way himself, often guided by his idealization of his "real father," which is an archetypal image. Siegfried does not even know his father's name; it is the one piece of information that Mime withheld to the end. Just as he has to forge a sword for himself, Siegfried also has to father himself and forge his own identity from fragmentary information, circumstances, and events.

SIEGFRIED

THE PSYCHOLOGICAL MEANING
OF THE DRAGON FIGHT

Killing a dragon who guards a treasure is what a hero is often called upon to do in myths and fairy tales. It tests his courage and strength and accomplishes something: he frees a princess, gets a treasure, or frees the land of a blight. Psychologically, he struggles with something that is destructive that could destroy him and others, kills off the power it has over him, frees something of great value in himself, and now can come into a positive relationship with an inner feminine and/or an outer woman.

The dragon fight can be with an addiction, regression, depression, or aggression, or any destructive complex in the psyche that keeps a person from growing. The dragon fight can also be enacted with real people who are intimidating, devouring, or abusive. Both men and women need to forge and hone a mental sword and decide if and when they will take on the fight. Some inner dragons must be fought because we are already in their grip, some stand in our way and prevent us from growing, and others lash out through us at others. Even when the dragon seems to be a real person or a chemical addiction, it is the susceptibility to be overcome by this kind of person or substance that makes it dangerous. Most dragon fights take place both within us and with whomever or whatever represents the dragon in the world.

Siegfried does not kill a generic dragon; he kills Fafner the dragon, who had been Fafner the giant. Fafner and Fasolt were the last of their race. They were skillful craftsmen and brothers who built Valhalla together, a task beyond the abilities of the gods. Fasolt was the more openhearted and trusting of the two. When the giants had been promised Freia as payment for building Valhalla, Fasolt wanted her beauty and grace to warm their household. Fafner, in contrast, recognized her great bargaining value, for without her the gods would lose their youthfulness. He prevailed when they accepted the Nibelung hoard as payment.

Motivated by his greed for riches and power, Fafner kills his brother Fasolt so he can have it all, the ring, the Tarnhelm, and the gold. Once they are in his possession, Fafner uses the Tarnhelm to change himself into a dragon. The physical shape he assumes reflects what had happened to his soul. His greed has made him inhuman, his features reflect his character, and being a dragon serves his sole purpose in life, which is to sit on the treasure and guard it.

Alberich puts a curse on the ring: that it will bring death to its lord, its wealth pleasure to no one, that care shall consume the man who commands it, and mortal envy those who covet it. His curse is psychologically true. The ring obsesses men who seek to have power over others and makes paranoid anyone who has possession of it.

Siegfried kills Fafner the dragon and Mime the dwarf. They represent two inner destructive possibilities. A person can become a "Fafner"—a mistrustful, miserly dragon and a social recluse—if he fears losing the wealth or power he has acquired. Such a man often takes pleasure in making others fearful, because it makes him feel powerful

SIEGFRIED

when he abuses his power and humiliates others. Or a man may become a fawning, devious "Mime" if he has been abused in the past and is afraid of those with power. However, a Mime the dwarf can become a Fafner the dragon, when he acquires an upper hand and can lord it over others, and vice versa.

Siegfried is not afraid of being devoured by the dragon or poisoned by Mime. He does not have any sense that either is a real danger to him. He realistically sizes up the dragon in a matter-of-fact way, trusts his strength and his sword, and has a strategy that he correctly assumes will work. He cannot learn fear under these circumstances, in which killing a dragon is part of a good day's work. Mime's motives and plot are transparently obvious to Siegfried, and with the same sword he rids himself of this companion. Symbolically, he disposes of the possibility of becoming paranoid or the possibility of staying in a hostile-dependent relationship just to have a companion.

In *The Valkyrie*, Brunnhilde directs Sieglinde to seek refuge from Wotan in the forest near Fafner's lair because "it is a place that Wotan fears and never goes near." Musing about why this was so then, and noting that Wotan as the Wanderer can approach the lair now led me to think about appropriate fear and appropriate avoidance, which self-knowledge provides. Sometimes, as was Siegfried's experience, killing a dragon is easy. Other times it is a long and difficult fight. And sometimes, one ought to avoid the vicinity of the dragon, because the dragon will probably get you if you venture into its neighborhood. This is the case when the power of an addiction or the power of an emotional complex is stronger than the ego's ability to resist, and we know and need to avoid the circumstances that put us at risk of succumbing.

Wotan's desire for the ring of power made it dangerous for him to go near the lair where Fafner guarded it. Especially, when he did not have control of his temper or addiction to power. Knowing that taking the ring by force will be his undoing, and the undoing of all the agreements he has made that brought order to his world might not be enough to deter him, for twice before he came close to paying an appalling price for power. As the Wanderer, Wotan is still focused upon the ring, though he is less identified with power himself and has taken on the appearance of the wise old man, which reflects the archetype in himself that is not susceptible.

It helps us to know what our particular dragon may be, so that we may be able to either take on the dragon fight or avoid the neighborhood where the dragon lurks. We need to assess what it is and why it is dangerous and what our fears and susceptibilities are that give it power. To take on a dragon fight successfully, we also need to find a hero with a sword within us—who can think clearly and be decisive.

When Siegfried tastes the dragon's blood, he symbolically takes into himself, or integrates, some essence of the experience, which changes him. He is now able to distinctly hear what the woodbird tells him and to act upon

SIEGFRIED

the information. He also can hear the truth hidden behind false words. In life, such is also the case. When we struggle with something that can destroy us—our addictions, obsessions and compulsions, a medical condition, or a destructive attitude—invariably we do more than defeat the foe; we get something positive as well that changes us.

SIEGFRIED FOLLOWS THE WOODBIRD

To follow the woodbird is like following an inner intuition or sense that calls you from one phase of your life to the next. You respond if you are unafraid, trusting that the direction you are taking is a true one for you. It is like hearing a true note or melody perfectly pitched for only you to hear, a song that you can follow if you choose to listen and trust your feelings, not knowing, really, where you are being led, or to whom you are going.

As he follows the woodbird, Siegfried is metaphorically in a time of transition. He is moving away from where he has been toward where he is fated to be next, from one phase of his life to the next, or one stage of psychological growth to the next. He has used the sword he forged himself to kill Mime and the dragon. As psychological metaphors, he decisively separated himself from the two emotional complexes that they represent: he will not become defensive and paranoid like the dragon, guarding treasures that he will never use; and he is free of Mime's manipulative deviousness. Symbolically, he has killed off the possibility of becoming like either of the significant negative figures in his childhood. Anyone who grows up in a dysfunctional family where power is the ruling principle needs to "kill off" the potential of becoming just like them before becoming truly free to go out in the world to meet his or her own destiny.

Siegfried also takes the treasure: two powerful symbols that he has yet to learn how to use. The ring of power is on his hand; the Tarnhelm is on his belt. With the one, he can rule others; with the other, he can transform himself into anything and will himself to be any place. In addition, he carries a sword that he knows how to use, and the taste of dragon blood enables him to hear the truth behind false words and hear the song of the woodbird that he is following.

INTUITIVE UNDERSTANDING

Growing up in households where people do not tell the truth about their feelings is, to use a telling medical word, "pathognomonic" of a dysfunctional family; that is, it is distinctly characteristic of this particular condition, without which one cannot make the diagnosis.

A child growing up in a dysfunctional family may correctly intuit the discrepancies between words and underlying feelings and then repress or suppress the information. When Mime offers Siegfried poison, Siegfried fully recognizes the deadliness of what he is being offered to quench his thirst. Though poison is a harsh metaphor, children in dysfunctional families or adult children from dysfunctional families need to recognize lies as poison; if swallowed, denials replace the truth of their own perceptions and feelings, and are as deadly to authenticity as a drink is to an alcoholic.

Siegfried spent his childhood in nature, which often has nurtured and given solace to children in dysfunctional families. A special hill or tree, a place near the river, a hidden nook in a garden may have been "home" to the soul of the child. Solitude in nature, daydreaming and listening to the birds as Siegfried did, allows us to hear our own thoughts and yearnings and to feel the truth of our own experience. It may even make us aware that we have a place in a benevolent and beautiful universe.

Only in solitude do we hear the voice of "the woodbird," a symbol of the inner voice or guidance that leads us toward our own spiritual and psychological unfolding. In the opera, the woodbird is a beautiful soprano voice. In the psyche, the woodbird is the voice of the soul. Siegfried follows the voice of the woodbird as long as he is alone. As soon as Wotan appears, the bird flies away. Wotan tells Siegfried that "the woodbird left to save its life!" When Wotan appears, Siegfried loses touch with the woodbird, which is what happens in all of us when we become arrogant, involved with exercising power, or engaged in conflict.

SUMMONING FEMININE WISDOM

Wotan as the Wanderer is an observing aspect of Wotan, who has wandered the earth searching for wisdom and now summons Erda, whom he calls the wisest of women, the all-wise one. The Wanderer is also a humbled aspect of Wotan, wearing a persona that does not command respect or fear. Mime's first impression of him is of an intrusive old man with whom he does not want to be bothered. To Siegfried, he is an annoying old fool with a missing eye. As the Wanderer, he is like King Lear, another wanderer, who discovered how insulated he had been from truth when he gave up his power. Kings and Wotans are authority figures with power over others. They usually do not hear the truth, because people are rightfully afraid to say what the king does not want to hear. Instead, they are deferred to and flattered, which makes authority figures susceptible to having an inflated sense of themselves, and a distorted view of reality.

In a patriarchal context, feminine wisdom, personified by Erda, has receded and is deep underground. She is a symbol of the part of the psyche that dreams and knows, tapping into the collective unconscious where past, present, and future are all one. The arrogant masculine intellect that assumes dominion over nature discounts the unconscious as irrational and meaningless. Loss of contact with dreams and depth results, as Erda recedes. This is what happens to individual men and women who assume that truth is only left-brain cognitive knowledge. When Erda disappears from consciousness, there is also a loss of contact with the mother realm that values relationships and nature.

Wotan awakens Erda only after he has wandered and inquired and has not found the wisdom he is seeking anywhere else. He comes to her at night, calling into a mountain cavern for her to rouse from slumber, an image that anyone who wants a significant dream can appreciate. When she heeds his summons and emerges, she glows with a bluish light that symbolizes a different kind of illumination. She comes up from the depths like archetypal dreams do, with mystery and numinosity and wisdom; if we value the dream, we need to brood upon its meaning until we get its wisdom.

Wotan wants to know "if the swift moving wheel can be stopped." Events set in motion by his desire for Valhalla and the forging of the ring have followed one upon the other. Wotan may be asking whether this karmic wheel can be stopped, or whether linear time itself and the effects of time can be stopped, or whether Erda can take away the cares and sorrow that have beset him since he became aware that his world will end. Erda's words, "all things that are perish," have haunted him.

There is a wisdom in this statement that reflects the course of nature, a consciousness of seasons and the inevitability of change, the knowledge that the earth has that all things die and go back to earth. This wisdom is resisted by men like Wotan, who build their equivalents of Valhalla that their influence may live forever. My clinical impression has been that awareness of death as an inevitability is denied or repressed as much as possible by power-oriented, control-seeking personalities, and that these efforts do not succeed very well. Fear of death and of aging, fear of waning power or loss of attractiveness, are frightening to a narcissistic person of either sex, who therefore notices every small indication of decline.

Wotan as the Wanderer has sought wisdom as his power to control events has waned. His appearance is that of the wise old man he needs to become. He struggles with his anger and his difficulty giving up power and the inevitable end. When he accepts that the end of his influence—the end of the gods—is fated, he denies that it causes him anguish and tells Erda that he has willed this end himself, that he gladly will yield his rule to the young. This is a stage in giving up control in which we say that what we cannot influence is how we willed it to be, and what we inevitably have to concede, we gladly intend, thus maintaining an illusion of control.

MENTOR-FATHER AND HERO-SON CONFRONTATIONS

Despite his earlier stated intent to Erda, Wotan does not voluntarily relinquish his power to Siegfried and instead blocks his way. This is a classic mentor-father and hero-son situation. Male mentors and their proteges notably come to this same impasse. A mentor or father who furthers a younger man's advancement often cannot bear to be surpassed by him; a confrontation then occurs with one or the other emerging as the victor, which also usually ends the relationship.

The mentor may resent the change in deference or idealization that happens when a younger man reaches the same level as his mentor, or is in line for his position, or has the possibility of surpassing him; he naturally no longer looks up to the mentor in the same way he did earlier. Fathers' sons, like fathers' daughters, go through a period of hero worship of their own fathers, which also usually happens with a mentor and is wonderfully gratifying to the older man. The time comes, however, for the younger man to become his own man rather than his mentor's man or an extension of his father, when he will put his own ideas forth, do things his own way, and come into his own. If the father or mentor is authoritarian and narcissistic, he experiences the younger person's normal healthy growth as a betrayal. The mentor-father's narcissistic rage and envy for opportunities the younger man has then causes his sudden devaluation of the younger man's character or ability which destroys the relationship.

A narcissistic father-mentor who finds that the younger man will not be an extension of his will may suddenly turn his back on his former protege, which happened to Siegmund, and may even deal the blow that is fatal to his career. Or he may find himself on the losing end of the confrontation with a Siegfried when he cannot bar his advancement.

A narcissistic father also becomes an internalized obstacle that prevents a son or daughter from succeeding or being creative. As Wotan bars the way with his spear, upon which are written binding agreements that ensure his power, so may adult-children of such fathers be stopped by binding emotional agreements. One such agreement might be to not surpass the father and become more successful than he is. Another agreement might be to fulfill a parent's ambition instead of choosing for oneself. In all dysfunctional families, there are agreements to remain silent about some subjects and emotions: these are the binding agreements that codependents enter with a Wotan with an addiction to power, rage, alcohol, gambling, or whatever it may be. To strike down these agreements in order to go on is what the hero in adult sons and daughters must do.

UNCONSCIOUS BRUNNHILDE

When Wotan summons Erda to advise him, she wants to know why he does not instead ask Brunnhilde, who is "courageous and wise." On hearing that Wotan has put Brunnhilde to sleep as punishment for defying him, Erda asks him some very searching questions.

If he (or the Wotan in all of us that is susceptible to being judgmental and hypocritical of others, especially our own children) were to take these questions to heart and not shirk from the answers, they could be stated and responded to like this:

- How can you punish our child for a fault of your own? Your example was the teacher.
- How can you punish our child for what she did? The feelings that she has heard you express influenced her to do what she did.

- How can you maintain that truth and justice are sacred to you and behave as you have? You lack integrity because your actions are not consistent with the values you believe in.

Wotan is in that highly ambivalent psychological situation of simultaneously wanting and not wanting to hear the truth. Like a psychoanalyst who indirectly confronts inconsistent behavior, Erda asks him questions.

Brunnhilde had indeed been courageous and wise, but this brought Wotan's wrath down upon her. She had disobeyed Wotan's will and obeyed his heart (for he loved Siegmund) and had been moved by her own compassion for Siegmund and Sieglinde to act against Wotan's orders. Love rather than obedience to authority guided her actions. She represents an ethical principle that places love above law or power and is a symbol of Wotan's anima or soul, which he punished and silenced, and hence can no longer consult.

Brunnhilde had the courage to defy Wotan's wrath when she aided Siegmund and Sieglinde. She also had the courage to step forward to face him when he accused her of being a coward afraid of facing her doom. However, she was not prepared for his punishment. That a father who "she thought loved her" would deliberately put her asleep, exposed, and vulnerable to the first man who came along (including a coward), who would take her virginity and be her master, was an appalling betrayal of parental love, a punishment beyond her imagination that could destroy her soul and spirit. Once a daughter feels the brunt of a narcissistic father's merciless rage and hostility, which can be in words or in physical or sexual abuse, she is changed. After hearing what Wotan plans as punishment for her, Brunnhilde is terrified and becomes timid, cajoling, and seductive in her efforts to persuade him to soften his punishment.

When punishment is terrifying, for self-preservation whatever provokes it must be suppressed. Wotan and Erda's daughter is indeed valiant and wise, but the punishment for behavior that is an expression of these qualities, makes it dangerous for her to be this way. In dysfunctional families, the positive strengths of daughters are often "put to sleep." Defenselessness results, predisposing them to become abused victims later.

AWAKENING BRUNNHILDE: AWAKENING TO FIRST LOVE

Siegfried crosses through the fire and sees a figure covered with a shield and wearing armor lying on a rock. Brunnhilde is the unconscious figure, but Siegfried is in a different way also unconscious. He has never seen a woman before or known that a woman could affect him.

Siegfried takes the shield and armor off the sleeping figure and gazes upon Brunnhilde. This affects him like the first pangs of falling in love, which for men commonly is in response to a woman's physical appearance. He is enchanted, a fiery blaze burns in his breast, his heart races, he feels anguish and yearning, he looks at her tenderly and is afraid;

then gladness charms fear from his heart, and he wants to touch and hold her, breathe her breath, and kiss her. When he does, he awakens Brunnhilde from her long sleep.

Brunnhilde awakens to see the sky and earth again, and once awake, she immediately asks, "Who is the man who wakes me to life?" In the first awakening to love, a woman usually wants to know who the man is through conversation and to place him in a context that she can relate to, which Brunnhilde does. She learns that his name is Siegfried, which moves her deeply. She recognizes him as the life she sheltered in Sieglinde's womb, that he is who she protected even before he was born. She has loved the image and idea that she had of who Siegfried would be and is ecstatic that it is he who awakens her now.

Siegfried confuses Brunnhilde with his mother, which is often psychologically true of a man's physical love for a woman; she is his lover, and he is lying with a woman who may be the age his mother was when he was an infant at her breast. If, like Siegfried, he was deprived of a mother's physical love, an untouched part of him yearns for contact with her body, and in lovemaking the woman is mother as well as lover.

Siegfried touches a corresponding maternal chord in Brunnhilde, who reaches out to him when he wonders if she could be his mother, asleep for all this time. She calls him an innocent child and tells him that she wants him to learn from her. She tells him that her love for him was the secret thought that she carried through her defiance of Wotan and her long sleep. She shows him her horse and her weapons and mourns the loss of her identity as a Valkyrie. While she talks, he grows increasingly passionate. She wants to talk; he wants to embrace her, and when he tries, she repulses him in terror and runs.

LOSS OF VIRGINITY AS A PSYCHOLOGICAL TRANSFORMATION

Brunnhilde loves Siegfried but is terrified of a physical consummation of her love, telling him that "wildly my fears seem to seize on me. Dreadful horrors arise in the dark." She proposes that he leave her in peace, keep the image of her with him, and "not destroy this maid who is yours."

Loss of virginity is a significantly different psychological experience for a woman than for a man. With first intercourse, she has a physical experience of being entered, of becoming vulnerable to the man, to pregnancy, to possible infection, to the unknown consequences of being forever changed. She feels instinct take his body over as he thrusts toward orgasm, and if she is sexually responsive this first time, she herself has the experience of being taken over by an orgasm. It is an initiatory experience that happens in her and that leaves her vulnerable. For many women, it is also an emotionally bonding act that increases their vulnerability. Historically, patriarchal societies have placed great value on virginity as a requirement for marriage, and any woman who lost her virginity under any circumstance other than marriage was ruined; once married, she belonged to this man forever as a possession. While this has changed, if there is a collective memory in the unconscious, it also has an influence. For these many reasons, loss of virginity can be a psychological experience that changes a woman's perception of herself and changes her life, especially for a Valkyrie, a warrior maiden who never before has felt vulnerable and unshielded.

To await the first man who awakens her and be from that moment slave to him as master is what Wotan told Brunnhilde would happen to her. Recall that Brunnhilde has been her father's confidante in an emotionally incestuous relationship in which she knows his weaknesses, and that she also has felt his fury, been terrified of him, and learned to plead and be conciliatory. This set of circumstances, in fact, prepares a woman to become a codependent in an abusive situation, to defer to and obey a man who treats her badly. Thus, Brunnhilde and women like her may rightfully fear what will happen to them when they have their first sexual relationship.

Loss of virginity for Siegfried and men like him is an experience of mastery rather than vulnerability. When Brunnhilde responds to him passionately, Siegfried notes, "I find again my boldness of heart; and what fear is I have failed to learn. My fear, I find, has faded and gone like a dream."

In their union, both Brunnhilde and Siegfried are ecstatic. Brunnhilde laughs as she says farewell to her previous life, farewell to Valhalla and to the gods, for she is no longer an immortal Valkyrie; now Siegfried is her "one and all." So it is archetypally, when a woman who has been a one-unto-herself virgin goddess and by loving becomes a vulnerable woman. There is "laughter in death" of her former self, and his.

BRUNNHILDE *puts the ring of the Nibelung on her finger, and rides onto Siegfried's funeral pyre, an act that ignites Valhalla and ends the old order. Truth is the fire that destroys and purifies dysfunctional relationships.*

TWILIGHT OF THE GODS
(GÖTTERDÄMMERUNG)

TRUTH BRINGS AN
END TO THE
CYCLE OF POWER

CAST OF CHARACTERS

The Norns: *three daughters of Erda, the goddess of wisdom, who weave the cord of destiny that determines fate*

Siegfried: *the hero, who killed the dragon, gained possession of the ring of the Nibelung, and awakened Brunnhilde; son of Siegmund and Sieglinde*

Brunnhilde: *the Valkyrie who lost her immortality when she disobeyed her father, Wotan, and lost her virginity when she was awakened by Siegfried and made his bride; daughter of Wotan and Erda*

Gunther: *a Gibichung mortal, ruler of a fiefdom on the Rhine, son of Gibich and Grimhild, brother of Gutrune, and half-brother to Hagen through their mother*

Gutrune: *a Gibichung mortal, sister of Gunther, half-sister of Hagen*

Hagen: *an illegitimate son of Alberich the Nibelung and Grimhild, half-brother to Gunther and Gutrune*

Waltraute: *a Valkyrie who tries to influence Brunnhilde*

Alberich: *the Nibelung dwarf who forged the ring of the Nibelung, had it taken from him by force, and is obsessed with repossessing it; father of Hagen*

Rhinemaidens: *three river nymphs who divulged the secret of the Rhinegold to Alberich, who stole it, and have been seeking its return to the river ever since*

Gibichung vassals and women

CHAPTER 4

TWILIGHT OF THE GODS

Truth Brings an End
to the Cycle of Power

The Story

THE PROLOGUE:

The three Norns—ancient goddesses—who weave the golden rope of destiny, are trying to fulfill their task, which has become increasingly difficult. They are Erda's daughters, and they spin and weave the wisdom that Erda dreams into existence. As they work, they go over the events that have changed forever, the order and harmony that they once knew.

The oldest Norn describes how they once did their spinning and weaving under the world ash tree, which was green and leafy. At the foot of the tree, there was a spring that was a source of wisdom. Wotan came to drink at this spring and paid for it by the loss of an eye. He broke a branch from this tree to make his spear, which wounded the tree, gradually weakening it, until it died. After that, the spring dried up.

The second, younger Norn takes up the thread of the story. She tells how Wotan made laws and treaties, which he carved into the shaft of the spear. With this spear, he ruled the world, until one day a hero broke his spear in two, destroying the power of Wotan's laws. Then the youngest Norn tells how Wotan ordered Valhalla's heroes to hack the trunk of the ash tree down, to cut its branches in pieces, and to pile this wood around Valhalla's walls. Wotan now sits on high in his hall with the immortals assembled around him. When the wood is set ablaze, the rule of the gods will be ended, and darkness will overtake them.

The Norns no longer have the world ash to tie the cord of destiny to. As they spin and sing stories of what has happened, they toss the rope from one to the other, unsuccessfully trying to tie it to rocks. The oldest Norn, who knows the past, complains that she no longer sees the sacred visions that Loge used to light up with his radiant fire. "What happened to him?" she asks. The second Norn tells her how Wotan controlled Loge with his spear and summoned him to surround Brunnhilde with his fire. The third Norn, who has knowledge of the future, describes how the fire will be summoned that will send Valhalla up in flames.

The cord is tangled and frayed. As its threads break against the jagged rocks, the second Norn, who has knowledge of the present, attributes this to the greed for power arising from the ring of the Nibelung and Alberich's curse.

The Norns scream, "It breaks! It breaks! It breaks!" as the rope divides. Recognizing that this marks their end, the Norns descend into the earth; they return to their mother, Erda, and disappear forever.

SIEGFRIED AND BRUNNHILDE PART

As the sun rises on Brunnhilde's rock, Siegfried and Brunnhilde are coming out of the cave. They have spent an indeterminate time together. He is wearing armor that she once wore and carries her shield as his own. She is seeing her beloved off to deeds of glory. Everything the gods had given her she has given him;

everything she was taught she has taught him. She has given all her wisdom and strength "to this man who is now my master," and her heart is full of love. As he is leaving, she says, "I fear that you may now despise me. I've no more to give."

Siegfried promises that he will remember Brunnhilde and remember that she loves him. Then, taking off the ring of the Nibelung, Siegfried gives it to her as a pledge of his love. Brunnhilde promises to guard the ring as long as she lives. She gives Siegfried her horse, Grane, who longs to fly through the clouds with her, but he lost this magic when Brunnhilde lost hers.

Siegfried promises Brunnhilde, "All my deeds will be your deeds"; "I am but Brunnhilde's arm." To which she responds, "I wish I were your soul, too!" Each pledges, "Apart, who can divide us? Divided, still we are one!"

THE GIBICHUNGS

Gunther, Gutrune, and Hagen are in the hall of the Gibichungs on the Rhine discussing their family fortunes. Gunther and Gutrune are brother and sister. Gunther is the ruler of this fiefdom. Hagen is their half-brother and the illegitimate son of their mother, Grimhild, and of Alberich the Nibelung. Hagen envies Gunther's legitimacy, while Gunther admires Hagen's cunning and personal power. Gunther asks Hagen to tell him if his fame along the Rhine is worthy of the Gibich name. Hagen responds that his fame is not great and suggests that it would be enhanced if he married well, and Gutrune did also.

When Gunther wants to know whom he should marry in order to increase his fame, Hagen tells him of Brunnhilde, the noblest woman in the world, and how she can be won only by Siegfried, the bravest of heroes, who killed the dragon and took possession of the Nibelung hoard and the ring of power. Gunther angrily retorts, "Why are you telling me about a treasure that I cannot have?!"

All Gunther has to do, Hagen says, is persuade Siegfried to win Brunnhilde as a bride for him. If Siegfried marries Gutrune, he could be persuaded to do this easily. Now Gutrune is upset: why would the bravest man in the world who could have the loveliest woman on earth choose her? "Remember the drink in the chest!" Hagen says conspiratorially. "We'll give him the magical drink, and he'll forget all women but you."

Conveniently, Siegfried is merrily seeking adventures and fame and is coming down the Rhine. He even seeks to meet the Gibichungs because he has heard of Gunther. We hear his horn sound. His boat docks, and Siegfried comes ashore.

Gunther welcomes Siegfried in peace and offers to share everything he has with him: his land, his vassals, and his hall. Siegfried reciprocates, saying that he, too, will share everything that he owns, but that his strength and his sword are all he possesses. Hagen questions this, asking, "What of the Nibelung gold? They say it belongs to you now."

Siegfried replies, "That treasure I quite forgot. I hold it of little worth and left it lying in a cavern." When Hagen asks, "You took no part of it?" Siegfried points to the Tarnhelm hanging from his belt, saying, "Just this piece, which I cannot use." Hagen tells him that it is the Tarnhelm, the Nibelung's most wonderful work, that if he puts it on his head he can transform himself into any shape, or if he wishes, it will take him any place he wants to go. "What else did you take from the cave?" Hagen asks. "Just a ring," Siegfried responds. "And where is it now?" inquires Hagen. "Kept safe on a fair woman's hand," Siegfried replies.

Gunther tells Siegfried that he does not need to give anything other than his friendship in return. Then Gutrune approaches, carrying a drinking horn, which she offers Siegfried. Raising the drinking horn to his lips, he remembers Brunnhilde and then drinks deeply. The potion takes immediate effect. He forgets Brunnhilde and becomes inflamed with passion for Gutrune. He is ardent and takes her hand. She blushes, becomes shy, and leaves, with Siegfried staring after her, entranced.

At this moment, Gunther speaks of the woman that he desires and cannot win. She is a maiden on a mountain surrounded by fire; only a hero who can go through the fire can make her his bride. Though he wants her, Gunther says that he cannot set foot on that mountain because he is afraid of the flames.

For a moment, Siegfried seems to be struggling with his memory, but this passes. Then he tells Gunther that because he is his friend—and if he can have Gutrune for his wife—he will win Gunther's bride for him. With a newfound cunning, Siegfried proposes to use the Tarnhelm to deceive Brunnhilde: "I can be changed into you." To cement this plan, Gunther and Siegfried pledge a blood brotherhood and set off up the Rhine. As they leave, Gutrune happily anticipates her wedding to Siegfried, and Hagen is pleased, for matters seem to be going according to plan.

BETRAYAL OF BRUNNHILDE

Brunnhilde is sitting at the cave entrance, thinking of Siegfried and kissing his ring, when she hears thunder and sees a dark cloud coming in her direction. A Valkyrie rides toward her—it is her sister Waltraute. Brunnhilde is overjoyed to see her coming, and wonders: did Waltraute break Wotan's command and come out of love? Has Wotan changed his mind and forgotten his anger? Is Waltraute here to gaze at Brunnhilde's rapture?

Much to the contrary, Waltraute comes in fear and anguish, seeking Brunnhilde's help to ward off disaster for the gods. She tells her how Wotan became the Wanderer and left Valhalla. He came back with his spear in splinters and had the heroes cut down the world ash and pile its pieces around the hall. Now he sits there silently, refusing the apples of youth, with the Valkyries gathered around his knees in fear. One day, Waltraute reminded him of Brunnhilde, and he sighed in grief and whispered, "If the Rhinemaidens got the ring from Brunnhilde, the curse will pass, and she will save both the gods and the world!"

Waltraute has come to plead with Brunnhilde to cast her ring into the Rhine. Brunnhilde refuses to part from the ring, saying that the ring tells her that Siegfried loves her, which means more to her than Valhalla and the eternal gods. Declaring that the ring will remain on her hand, Brunnhilde sends Waltraute away.

Alone once more, Brunnhilde notes that her guardian flames are flaring up. She hears a horn and recognizes it as Siegfried's. Joyfully, she goes to greet him and is terrified when a strange man appears instead. He wears the Tarnhelm and looks like Gunther. He tells her that has come to claim her and will overpower her if she resists. Brunnhilde now understands Wotan's punishment and the shame and sorrow it will bring her. The man wants to take her into her cave and make her obey him. Feeling that Siegfried's ring will protect her, she threatens him with it, saying, "No mortal brings me to shame as long as this ring is my guard!"

The ring does not protect Brunnhilde. The man grabs her, and they struggle. She wrenches free, and he catches her again, and as she screams, he forces the ring from her finger and puts it on his own. "Now you are mine, Brunnhilde, Gunther's bride. We shall stay in your cave." Beaten and trembling, she goes into the cave as he commands, expecting to be raped.

Siegfried follows her, draws his sword, and asks Notung to witness how he keeps his vow to his brother. Then saying to it, "Part me now from Gunther's bride!" he enters the cave.

ALBERICH APPEARS TO HAGEN

It is night, and Hagen sits in front of the Gibichung hall apparently sleeping, his spear on his arm, his shield at his side. His

TWILIGHT OF THE GODS

father, Alberich, crouches before him, leaning his arms on Hagen's knees, and talks softly to him. Hagen listens and responds. It is a dreamlike scene, illuminated only by the moon. It could be a dream or an interior conversation.

Alberich is there to urge his son to get possession of the ring. "You were bred so that you'd fight my enemies," he tells him, and the time is now. Raised to hate, Hagen is a man who says of himself that he was "old as a youth, hated the happy, and was never glad." While Alberich tries to make Hagen swear that he will win the ring for him, Hagen swears he will get it but says it will be his and to trust him and not fear. As Alberich disappears, he urges Hagen to "be true! Be true!"

SIEGFRIED RETURNS

It is sunrise. Hagen has not changed position and is apparently asleep. Suddenly Siegfried appears nearby, announcing his return with a great shout, and startles Hagen awake. Siegfried tells Hagen that he won Brunnhilde, and now she and Gunther are coming by boat down the Rhine, while he used the Tarnhelm to wish himself here and arrived immediately. Gutrune joins them to hear how Siegfried had gone through the fire to win Brunnhilde for Gunther. Because of the Tarnhelm, no one can tell them apart, and as Gunther he had spent the night with Brunnhilde.

Gutrune wants to know what happened between them, asking if he "mastered the courageous maiden."

Siegfried replies, "She felt—Gunther's might."

"Was she married to you, then?" is Gutrune's next question.

"She obeyed her rightful husband for a full and marital night," he responds.

Gutrune gets more specific and now asks, "Did you pass as rightful spouse?"

To which he says, "I was faithful to Gutrune."

Gutrune accepts his statement of faithfulness. However, a listener less eager to believe him could come to the opposite conclusion. If, as Gunther, Siegfried had forced sex upon Brunnhilde, this would have been marital rape and a betrayal of Gunther and Gutrune as well as Brunnhilde.

GUNTHER COMES HOME WITH BRUNNHILDE

When the sails of the boat bearing Gunther and Brunnhilde are seen at a distance, Gutrune directs Hagen to summon the vassals to prepare a splendid welcome for them. Hagen climbs a high rock and sounds the horn, calling the vassals to awaken and come with their weapons.

The men arrive with their weapons, singly and in groups, asking "What is the danger?" "Who is the foe?"

Hagen tells them that Gunther is coming with his fiery wife and that he was aided by his friend Siegfried, who saved him from harm. "Is he pursued by furious kinsmen?" they ask.

"No one is in pursuit," Hagen assures them. They are to use their weapons to slaughter sacred animals as offerings and to fill their drinking horns with wine. At this good news, they break into laughter and are quieted by Hagen, who tells them to prepare to receive Gunther and his wife, Brunnhilde, and that they must honor her, come to her aid, and revenge her if she is wronged.

When they arrive, Gunther steps out of the boat with Brunnhilde, who obediently follows him. Her eyes are downcast, her demeanor defeated. Gunther's vassals hail and welcome them. Gunther presents her to them as a prize: "No man could win a nobler woman. The Gibichungs have been blessed; to new renown we rise today!"

Meanwhile, Siegfried and Gutrune come out to welcome them, accompanied by women attendants. Gunther greets them, saying, "Two pairs in wedlock shall be blessed here."

TWILIGHT OF THE GODS

Bringing Brunnhilde forward, he says, "Brunnhilde and Gunther, Gutrune and Siegfried!"

Hearing Siegfried's name, Brunnhilde looks up, greatly startled. She gazes fixedly at him and begins to tremble violently. Brunnhilde is scarcely able to control herself as she repeats their names, "Siegfried . . . here? Gutrune . . . ?"

Siegfried tells Brunnhilde that he has won Gunther's gentle sister, as Gunther has won Brunnhilde.

Brunnhilde is intensely affected by this statement and accuses Siegfried of lying. Then, realizing that he does not recognize her, she becomes further distressed. Siegfried turns to Gunther to calm Brunnhilde, which Gunther cannot do. Instead, her hysteria grows when she sees the ring on Siegfried's hand; she points to it accusatorially. Her behavior alarms the vassals. They wonder why she is reacting to Siegfried and the ring as she is.

At this point, Hagen steps forth from the crowd, saying, "Mark her words; let her charge be heard!"

Brunnhilde sees Siegfried wearing the ring that "Gunther" had forcibly taken from her. "How did you get the ring from his hand?" she asks Siegfried, pointing to Gunther. Siegfried looks at the ring and says he did not get it from him. Now Brunnhilde turns to Gunther, demanding that he claim it as his right. "Make him return the ring!" This perplexes Gunther, who says he did not give Siegfried anything—"Are you sure it is yours?" When Gunther cannot account for the ring, Brunnhilde turns on Siegfried and announces that he stole it from her. She denounces him as a traitor and a thief.

Confusion mounts. Siegfried denies that he took the ring from a woman's hand and insists that he won it himself when he fought Fafner. Hagen intervenes, once more focusing the crowd's attention upon Brunnhilde's anguished accusations: "Betrayed! Betrayed! Shamefully betrayed! How can I be revenged?"

Gutrune and the vassals ask, "By whom?" Brunnhilde calls to the immortal gods, whose decrees have brought her such grief and shame, to hear her petition for vengeance and death to her betrayer.

Then Brunnhilde turns to the crowd, saying, "All of you, hear me: not Gunther but Siegfried made me his wife!" The crowd is aghast. If this accusation is true, Siegfried is a traitor who has dishonored and shamed Gunther and been unfaithful to Gutrune. Siegfried defends himself, saying that he kept his word by placing Notung between himself and Gunther's unhappy wife. Brunnhilde retorts that he lies, that she knows of his sword's sharpness, but she also knows of its scabbard, in which it slept all night on the wall.

Gunther says that he is disgraced unless Siegfried will "swear that she lies!" Gutrune also demands to be assured that "all she says is a lie!" The vassals demand that Siegfried answer the charge and swear it on a spearpoint.

Hagen now offers his spear as witness to the vow. He holds out his spear to Siegfried, who touches the point with two fingers of his right hand. Invoking the spear to defend his honor, Siegfried swears, "If I acted falsely, let this spear strike my heart. If what she says is true and I betrayed my brother, let this spear kill me."

Brunnhilde angrily tears Siegfried's hand away from the spearpoint, replacing it with her own. She calls upon the spear to strike him and kill him for his treachery, swearing that he has betrayed every vow and now has sworn falsehood. The vassals are in an uproar; for a woman to do this is unheard of. Siegfried now patronizes Brunnhilde, and, speaking man to man to Gunther, suggests that he grant her time and rest to get over being upset. He is sorry that the deception was not successful and suspects that it was a failing of the Tarnhelm. Then, telling Gunther that "Brunnhilde will soon learn to love you and will thank me as well," he lightheartedly puts his arm around Gutrune and leads the vassals and women to the wedding feast.

TWILIGHT OF THE GODS

DECIDING SIEGFRIED'S DEATH

Gunther, Hagen, and Brunnhilde remain behind, while all the others follow Siegfried and Gutrune. Brunnhilde is torn by fury and anguish and cries out for vengeance. Hagen offers to kill Siegfried, but Brunnhilde says this is impossible because she wove a spell to protect him from his enemies. However, assuming that he would never turn his back on an enemy and flee, she did not protect his back. Hagen tells her that his spear now knows where to strike.

In the meantime, Gunther is feeling very sorry for himself and overwhelmed with shame. Brunnhilde, contemptuous of him, calls him a coward because he feared the flames, let Siegfried win her, and then dared to claim her. When Gunther pleads with Hagen, "Help! Save my honor!" adding, "Help for our mother, for you, too, are her son!" Hagen tells him that only Siegfried's death can purge his shame. Brunnhilde adds that Siegfried's death will atone for his crime and for Gunther's.

Then Hagen takes Gunther aside and tells him that he will do the deed, and Gunther will gain the ring. With the ring, Hagen promises that "all the world will be yours to command"; this decides Gunther and seals Siegfried's doom. However, Gunther is concerned that Siegfried's death will dismay Gutrune because she loves him (while Brunnhilde curses her for being an enchantress and stealing him), so the deed will need to be concealed. Hagen agrees and plans an accident: "Our hero runs on ahead: we'll find him killed by a boar."

Having decided Siegfried's death, Gunther and Brunnhilde call upon the gods for help, to Wotan the lord of vows and god of revenge, and all the feared heavenly host. Hagen invokes his Nibelung father, Alberich.

Then the bridal procession comes toward them. Gunther and Brunnhilde are soon surrounded by the celebrants. The men carry Siegfried on a shield and Gutrune on a chair. The women invite Brunnhilde to accompany them, and Gutrune smiles at her invitingly. Brunnhilde is about to refuse, when Hagen intervenes and forces her toward Gunther, who seizes her hand, and they take their places in the bridal procession.

THE RHINEMAIDENS AND SIEGFRIED

It is the day after the wedding celebration. The scene has shifted to the wilderness, through which the Rhine is flowing. The three Rhinemaidens have risen to the surface of the river to enjoy the sunlight. They call upon the sun to send them the hero who can give them back the Rhinegold.

Preceded by the sound of his horn, Siegfried comes to the river by himself. He became separated from the others in the hunting party when he followed a bear. When he sees the Rhinemaidens, he teases them: "Did they entice the bear away? Was he their playmate?"

"Will he give them a reward, if they find his bear?" the Rhinemaidens want to know, bantering with Siegfried to give them the golden ring on his finger. When he says that his wife would scold him if he gave them the ring, they treat him scornfully, laugh at him, and then dive down and temporarily disappear. Their scorn tempts him to do what they ask. He takes off the ring, calls to them, and, holding it high, says that he will give them the ring if they come back.

When the Rhinemaidens return, they are solemn. They see Siegfried holding the ring and tell him how it was cursed by Alberich, and that he is doomed if he keeps it: "You die today unless you give the ring to our care," they warn. Siegfried takes this as a challenge, saying that "if you had smiled the ring would be yours," but now, even if it were worthless, he would not give it to them.

They say farewell to Siegfried, observing he once was wise but is wise no more, that he threw away a glorious gift and holds on to the ring that will doom him. As they leave, they tell him, "You die today, and your ring returns to Brunnhilde; by her, our prayer will be heard."

Siegfried watches the Rhinemaidens go, thinking that he has learned about women: "If smiles don't work, they threaten you, and if you scorn their threats, they scold." And yet, "Were I not Gutrune's husband, I'd try to capture one of those pretty maids—make her mine!"

SIEGFRIED'S DEATH

Siegfried hears the calls of the hunting party and answers with his horn. Hagen and Gunther find him, and, followed by the vassals, all join Siegfried. They bring food and drink with them. Siegfried tells them lightheartedly how he followed a bear and found the frolicking Rhinemaidens, who warned him that he would find his death today. At hearing this, Gunther shudders.

As the men rest, eat, and drink, Hagen wonders about the rumors that Siegfried can understand the talk of birds. Siegfried says that it is true, "But since women have sung their songs to me, I've no longer cared for birdsong." Then, at Hagen's urging, he reminisces about his youth, about Mime, about forging Notung from the fragments of his father's broken sword, about killing the dragon, and about how he was warned of Mime's treachery by the woodbird and killed him.

At this point in his story, Hagen gives Siegfried a fresh drink and adds an herb that restores memory. Now Siegfried tells them of going through the fire to find his glorious bride, Brunnhilde, asleep in shining armor, of how he kissed his bride awake and was held in her lovely arms. He continues as he did before, with no thought about the effect on his listeners of what he is saying.

At hearing this, Gunther springs to his feet in dismay, for Siegfried reveals to everyone that Brunnhilde was his before

Gunther married her. At that moment, two ravens fly up out of a bush, cry out, and circle over Siegfried's head before flying away. Hagen asks if Siegfried can tell what the ravens said. At this, Siegfried stands up suddenly, saying, "Vengeance! That's what they cry!" As he turns his back on Hagen to watch them fly off, Hagen thrusts his spear into Siegfried's back. Gunther seizes his arm as if to pull him out of danger, but it is too late. Siegfried is mortally wounded, and he falls.

The deed done, Hagen walks away. Gunther becomes grief stricken, and others support Siegfried in a sitting position. As he is dying, Siegfried calls to Brunnhilde, his "holiest bride," to awaken. He speaks of her as if she is there with him, and his face is radiant. Then he sinks back and dies.

GUTRUNE RECOGNIZES THE TRUTH

At the Gibichung hall, Gutrune is restless. She has awakened from a bad dream and wishes Siegfried were back. Hearing Hagen's voice, she has a premonition of fear. Hagen enters the hall to announce Siegfried's return, followed by the procession bearing his body into the hall. Hagen tells Gutrune that Siegfried is dead, slain by a ferocious boar. She cries out and falls on Siegfried's body, accusing Gunther of murder, which he denies, saying it was Hagen who killed Siegfried with his spear. Gunther curses Hagen, who defiantly takes credit for the death and by this right claims the ring. Gunther declares that it is his and also claims it for Gutrune. Hagen and Gunther fight. Hagen kills Gunther and reaches for the ring on Siegfried's hand.

At that moment, Siegfried's hand and arm rise straight up. The women cry out, and everyone is frozen in terror at the sight. Then Brunnhilde walks into the scene, saying that she hears no cries for the dead hero. At this, Gutrune blames her for arousing the men against him and bringing shame on their house. With calm authority in her voice, Brunnhilde tells

Gutrune that she was only Siegfried's mistress, while she—Brunnhilde—was his true wife, and that "Siegfried and Brunnhilde were one."

Gutrune recognizes that she is hearing the truth and curses Hagen: she had followed his advice and had given Siegfried the drink that made him forget Brunnhilde. Now, in sorrow and shame, she turns away from Siegfried and bends over Gunther's body in grief.

THE END OF THE GODS

Brunnhilde turns to the assembled vassals, ordering them to build a funeral pyre with huge logs, so that a great fire will leap into the sky.

As the vassals build the pyre, Brunnhilde gazes at Siegfried's body, absorbed in her thoughts and transfigured. She eulogizes Siegfried for his purity and faithfulness, even in his error and betrayal: "He was the truest, and there was none more false." Looking upward, she asks, "Do you know why that was?"

Brunnhilde now addresses Wotan: "By his most valiant deed he fulfilled your desire, but he was forced to share in your curse—that curse that has doomed you." She tells him that because Siegfried betrayed her, she in her grief has grown wise. Now she knows what must be.

Brunnhilde takes the ring from Siegfried's hand, places it on her finger, and promises the Rhinemaidens that they can reclaim their treasure from the ashes. Then she directs Wotan's ravens to summon Loge to burn Valhalla as she casts the torch into the pyre. At this point in the opera, Wagner's orchestral music alone conveys Brunnhilde's feelings and the meaning of what she is doing.

Though there are no words, and everything is expressed through the magnificence of the music, Wagner did write lines for Brunnhilde but did not set them to music: in them, Brunnhilde addresses the people who will remain after the race of gods are gone and bequeaths to them "my wisdom's holiest hoard": "Not goods, nor gold, nor house, nor hearth, nor empty treaties, nor false tradition's pitiless law: blessed in joy and in sorrow, I bequeath only love!"

Brunnhilde flings the torch on the pyre, which blazes upward, calling on Loge, the fire god, to take the fire to Valhalla, where Wotan waits for the end. She then mounts her horse, Grane, whom she greets as her friend. Grane carries Brunnhilde into the flames as she calls out: "Siegfried! Siegfried! Brunnhilde greets you as wife!" The music is ecstatic, celebrating a consummation, a union of the two who now will be as one in death or through death. Siegfried's theme, her Valkyrie music, and the motif of redemption by love come together.

When the fire subsides, a huge flood overflows the Rhine. The three Rhinemaidens are riding a huge wave that appears above the extinguished pyre. Hagen becomes alarmed at seeing them, throws off his armor, and plunges madly into the flood, crying, "Give me back the ring!" He is drawn downward into the depths by two of the Rhinemaidens, while the third joyfully holds up the regained ring. Meanwhile, in the heavens, Valhalla is ablaze in the sky.

The old order passes, and, purified by Brunnhilde's sacrifice, a new era can begin.

Truth Brings an End to the Cycle of Power

THE GIBICHUNGS — GUNTHER AND GUTRUNE — ALBERICH'S son Hagen, Siegfried, and Brunnhilde cross destinies in

TWILIGHT OF THE GODS

Twilight of the Gods. They are all "adult children" in roles their power-seeking dysfunctional families prepared them for. Their fate is a consequence of what happens when circumstance interacts with character. They turn out to be quite familiar—as types of people or aspects of people who grow up in patriarchal families, where ambition and acquisition are more important than love.

THE STATUS SEEKERS: THE GIBICHUNGS

The Gibichungs live on the Rhine in a large hall, with serfs and servants. Gunther is the ruler of this minor fiefdom. He wants to increase his family fame and discusses how to do it with his sister and half-brother. Gunther in contemporary clothing resembles the social climber who inherits some wealth and ambition and consults an image maker about what he can do to increase his own and his family's prestige. Gunther is advised to marry upward, and his sister Gutrune should as well, if he wants to make the family name more well known.

Gunther is ambitious for fame. Wanting to be more famous than he is already was also one of Wotan's reasons for building Valhalla. Fame has to do with the persona, with how we look to others. Like all other kinds of power, it is coveted, compensates for a lack of love, distances us from others, and makes it possible to feel superior and get our way.

The persona or face we put on to meet the world comes from the theater of classical Greece. A *persona* was the mask worn to signify who the actor was playing; persona was consistent with character and helped the audience to understand what they were witnessing; used thusly, it revealed rather than hid. A persona can still be an honest statement, a social face that truly reflects who we are, made up of how we look, talk, dress, and behave.

A persona can also be a mask, deliberately used to deceive or cover up who we really are; then it is a construct or false self that is presented to the world as if it were real.

Dysfunctional families often encourage children to be overly concerned with their personas; what people think of them is more important to such parents than what their children really feel. Required to put on a false face to hide the truth that theirs is anything other than a perfect family, children are expected to lie, and they often cling to the lie and repress the truth.

Gunther and Gutrune are called the Gibichungs. Their father, Gibich, established the family name. Hagen's father is Alberich the Nibelung, who forged the ring. They have the same mother, who was bought by Alberich for gold. With this family history, it is no wonder that they can calculatedly decide who to marry for status and then plan to deceive and manipulate them in order to bring this about. If Brunnhilde is "the noblest woman in the world," she becomes a very desirable acquisition as a wife for Gunther. If Siegfried is "the greatest hero," then as Gutrune's husband he will add luster to the Gibichungs. Personal feelings do not matter: neither those of their intended spouses nor their own, even for something as personal as marriage. When fame or power is the most important consideration, then marriage is a matter of barter, sale, alliances, and property, not love.

The persona orientation that the Gibichungs have is seen in adults who as children were expected to reflect well on their parents. Marrying well when it is time to marry is commonly done. The right marriage with the large social wedding is something the adult child may do for his parents, not for himself (or herself). Though at the time, it may seem to be a personal choice, emotional needs are often not really considered. Enviable social alliances are not a basis for real intimacy.

Gutrune is an example of the woman who has inner doubts that a socially desirable man could love her: "You mock me, cruel Hagen, for how could Siegfried love me?". She will use whatever she can to attract him, and once he is in love or infatuated with her through her manipulations, she is momentarily happy. She will overlook his behavior and her doubts, as Gutrune did on hearing about Brunnhilde and Siegfried's use of the Tarnhelm, in order to be married to a man who gives her status and compensates for her lack of self-esteem. As an adult child, she is motivated to please her parents (who may by now be inner figures), and, by doing this, she hopes to get their love and approval.

Gunther is also an example of a man who chooses a wife with a total disregard for feelings, his own or Brunnhilde's. He seeks her because he is told she is the best match he can find, and he uses deception to get close to her. Once she is vulnerable, he takes advantage of it and brings her home as a trophy to bring esteem to his family.

Gunther is a coward who cannot go through the fire or kill; he lacks both courage and cold-bloodedness. He is an unprincipled person who willingly follows stronger personalities, led by his own opportunistic motives. Appearances matter, not real feelings or actions. Thus he can acquiesce to the murder of his new brother-in-law and then be concerned that they preserve appearances with Gutrune, whom he thinks loves Siegfried. Feelings, this time hers, are not taken into consideration.

Gunther, like Hagen and Siegfried, does not feel empathy for others, nor does he feel much himself, except for shame, which he feels deeply. How he appears in the eyes of others is what matters. Wanting fame motivates him at the beginning; avoiding shame now becomes the overriding concern. For Gunther shame is not an inner experience in which he has behaved shamefully in his own eyes but a public humiliation in which he looks bad to others.

Gunther and Gutrune's outer-oriented psychology is present in adult children of dysfunctional families that are much more concerned for what the neighbors think than what their children feel, and who make their children responsible for keeping up a family persona. However, Gunther's particular psychology, in which he is overwhelmed by shame that people will know that Siegfried has had a sexual relationship with his wife (for whom Gunther has no personal feelings) and his willingness to see him murdered is like that of children who feel terrible shame for the sexual activities of their parents and have a murderous anger buried in them.

When Gunther turns in desperation to Hagen and says, "Help, Hagen! Save my honor! Help for our mother, for you, too, are her son!" his words tie his dishonor to her, and we recall that Alberich "bought her with gold" in order to have a son. Known as illegitimate, Hagen has even more reason to be shamed, but deadly hate dominates him. Children are greatly vulnerable to shame through the sexual behavior of a mother or harm to her honor. As the property of her husband, he would be the one who sold her and dishonored her; if he were dead and she sold herself, his memory would be dishonored; in either case, Gunther feels shame for the dishonor to his mother and the family name and tried unsuccessfully to redeem them through these marriages. Instead, the family shame and his own have suffered further. When a parent shames a child by his or her behavior and humiliates him, that child will have an acute sensitivity to shame as an adult.

THE WEAPON OF VENGEANCE
AND HATRED: HAGEN

Hagen is to be Siegfried's murderer, and yet, on hearing the dialogue between him and his father, Alberich, I could not help but feel "poor Hagen" for the boy he once was. His childhood prepared him to be an assassin, a terrorist, or whatever it took to be an instrument of his father's vengeance and a means through which his father could acquire the ring of power. Hagen was bred to hate and schooled to carry out his father's will. Consequently, he was never happy and envied those who were. He was a child who was always old, as children are when they are not allowed a childhood.

Alberich had renounced love for power. His sole obsession was to regain the ring. For this he bought Hagen's mother and fathered this son. Alberich's psychology is that of a coldly calculating fanatic, whose hatred arises from abuse, deprivation, humiliation, and a burning intensity for vengeance—which protects him psychologically from grief and from feeling insignificant. He will even the score in the next generation through his son. Currently, in the Israeli, Palestinian, Arab cauldron of hatred in the Middle East, camps and households are shaping such sons of vengeance. Burning hatreds carried on by successive generations are part of history.

To Alberich and other fathers who are obsessed with vengeance, a son has no legitimate needs of his own. He is to be the means for his father to have his needs met. He exists to redeem the deep narcissistic wounds his father suffered. He will make up for his father's humiliation and insignificance by acquiring the power that will enable the father to humiliate his enemies—even if it takes the biblical three generations. To please his father as well as in fear of him, a son carries out his father's will with his life, hoping that if he does that his father will love him and that by doing what his father needs him to do, he will heal his father's wounds as well.

In the emotional confusion of a dysfunctional family, a child may accurately hear and respond to a parent who is saying, "If you love me, you will be who I need," while that same parent totally disregards the legitimate needs of his (or her) child for adequate parenting. Alberich tells Hagen, for example, "Cherish that hatred! Then you will love your unhappy, joyless father, as you should!"

Hagen was totally abandoned emotionally, as children are whose feelings have been not only disregarded but also actively rejected. In making a son an instrument of his vengeance, through whom he can get even or triumph over an enemy who humiliated him, a father actively suppresses (through the use of ridicule and corporal punishment) a child's expression of fear or sympathy or complaints of any kind. Such a father acts as if he were a marine drill instructor and his son a raw recruit. When the son "shapes up," it costs him his childhood and his emotional development; he becomes focused, tough, unfeeling, and proud of it. Inside, however, there is an abandoned child who is deeply envious of those very people he treats with contempt for being soft.

The one part of the child that does develop is his intelligence (and whatever other "warrior" skill matters to the father, which could be athletic ability, academic excellence, or military or terrorist skills). A child learns to observe a punitive parent very closely, to think before he says or does anything, and to keep his thoughts to himself. He becomes unspontaneous, "a child who was always old," a loner who hides his loneliness and envy of others who belong from himself by his superior and contemptuous attitude.

THE OPPORTUNIST: SIEGFRIED

Siegfried leaves Brunnhilde to seek adventure and fame. While Siegfried's arrival plays into the Gibichung plans, it is Siegfried who seeks them out and they who are reflections of the shallowness of his inner life. He is a famous hero just barely out of the woods, impressed by the signs of Gibichung wealth and property and flattered by Gunther's manipulatively intended generous offer of friendship. Attractive, sophisticated Gutrune then offers him a drinking horn containing a potion, and he drinks it.

The last time Siegfried was offered a poisoned drink, it was from Mime. Then he could hear the truth behind the deceptive words, know the ulterior motives, and refuse the drink. Though he has the ability to "hear" the truth—as we all do—this time he does not listen. We often discount intuition, especially in situations like this, in which the people we should mistrust have such impressive personas and charming words.

Siegfried is taken in by the Gibichungs and drinks the potion that makes him forget Brunnhilde, fall in love with Gutrune, and fall into Gunther's plans. Without the need of a potion to explain it, a similar sequence of events often occurs in the lives of talented and ambitious men, the heroes on the way up. On finding that they are welcomed into a group of sophisticated or affluent people, they may forget the sweetheart or wife who would not fit into this new group and forsake the values she represents. Enamored with a new image of himself, he becomes infatuated with a woman who belongs to the group he now aspires to be part of and forgets the woman who loves him and, like Brunnhilde, helped get him the education and the equivalent of horse and armor to go into the larger world. He forgets her in his heart, forgets the man he used to be. Chameleonlike, a Siegfried takes on the appearance of Gunther as he makes his persona over to fit into this new group or class.

The wife who saw her husband through medical school and residency and is left by him when he completes his training is a cliche—because she is so common. While there are reasons that have to do with the training and individualized personal situations that cause this to happen, opportunism can also play a part. He has gone through an arduous training that makes him a "hero" and is now a man that a "Gutrune," who wants to marry a doctor, finds attractive. He, in turn, is welcomed into a status-conscious affluent world toward which he may have aspirations. If this is so, he may be drawn to a woman who matches his new status, who in his eyes is a more appropriate "doctor's wife" than the working woman who made it possible for him to become a doctor. A classic film, *Room at the Top*, chronicles the rise of an ambitious man from a working-class background who has an opportunity to marry the boss's daughter but needs to be rid of the devoted woman in his life, and he plots to kill her. Usually the killing act is metaphorical, not literal.

Siegfried easily betrays his anima and the woman who loves him. His dysfunctional family prepared him to be this way. Mime manipulated and used him, making him susceptible to being used and to using others. There are opportunist "Gibichungs" everywhere. They are also common influential inner figures in the psyches of people raised in families that care more about their own status than their children's feelings. These children become narcissistic adults who continue to discount what they feel and do not feel for others, which makes it easy for them to be opportunists manipulated by other opportunists.

SIEGFRIED AND THE TARNHELM: THE CHAMELEON

When Siegfried learns what the Tarnhelm is good for, he takes to its use immediately. He proposes and carries out his plan to appear to Brunnhilde as Gunther. Siegfried has entered a social world that he could be part of, drinks the potion, and discovers he can change his appearance and go anywhere he wishes. Looked at metaphorically, the Tarnhelm gives him the power to take on any persona that will advance his ambitions, and the ability to do this can take him anywhere he wants to go. The potion lets him forget anyone who once mattered to him and be superficially in love with whomever or whatever attracts him. These are the qualities that make a person chameleonlike when he or she is an attractive, bright person, exceedingly seductive, and thus successful at first impressions.

Siegfried went from being a nobody in a cave with a dwarf for a parent to being a hero who has slain a dragon with the sword he forged himself. He enters the social world as the hero of the moment (as sport champions or war heroes can become), and is looked upon by the Gibichungs as a man who will enhance their status. In their company, he completely forgets Brunnhilde, and learns how to use the Tarnhelm. Psychologically, he is a fearless man with no family or emotional ties, a heroic reputation, and no connection to his soul or anima. He lacks depth and has no loyalties, can change his persona when it serves him and fit in anywhere he wishes, and has been drawn to the company of people for whom fame and appearances matter.

In Siegfried the adult, there is the deprived and lonely child who went through the woods, blowing his horn, hoping to attract a friend. The child in him followed the woodbird, still yearning to find a friend and wondering what it would be like to have a mother. It was this adult child who came to Brunnhilde, took everything she had to offer, and then went out to seek adventure and fame. This adult child was also in search of a male friend and found to his happiness that Gunther welcomed him, made him a blood brother, and offered him his sister.

Siegfried is like a self-centered child with no idea how deeply a woman might be affected by his betrayal and loss because it is beyond his developmental grasp. Siegfried, like most adult children of dysfunctional families, is out of touch with his own feelings because no one valued them at best and punished him for expressing them at worst. He cannot empathize with others, in part because he does not know much about feelings and because Mime hid his true feelings from him and told him lies. As a child, Siegfried was not genuinely loved and was consistently lied to about being loved. Words about feelings were used to manipulate him, and he never experienced how words, emotion, and body language come together when feelings are authentically expressed.

The chameleonlike person learns how to be pleasing and manipulative. He or she adapts himself or herself to those around him, often unconsciously. It is a surface adaptation that does not reflect any depth of feeling.

THE OBEDIENT AND PASSIVE PLEASER: BRUNNHILDE AS A VICTIM OF ABUSE

When Brunnhilde comes to the Gibichung hall, she is despondent, her eyes downcast. She walks behind Gunther and is passive and compliant, an unresisting captive being welcomed as Gunther's new bride. At this point she is in a numbed depression and is going along with what is expected of her. Her demeanor and behavior are those of a woman who has been violated and is not yet in touch with her feelings. She also behaves like an obedient child in a dysfunctional family, who is stunned and helpless after being traumatized.

What has happened to Brunnhilde has parallels in everyday life. When she disobeys Wotan and tries to save Siegmund, his wrath and the punishment he decrees are devastating. She had been her father's favorite child, and

TWILIGHT OF THE GODS

until that moment she had seen love, pride, and tenderness in his eyes, which now look at her with hatred and fury. Sexual jealousy and impotency and his mistaken assumptions (his projection) that she think him weak fuel a rage that is terrifying in its intensity and destructiveness. Further, he tells her that he will abandon her forever and leave her to be sexually violated and thereafter dominated by the first man who finds her.

In ordinary life, children are too often the recipients of impotent rage and fury from a parent on whom a child depends for protection; that parent may hurl terrible accusations at the child that are beyond her or his comprehension; the parent may promise punishments every bit as terrifying to the child as Wotan's was to Brunnhilde. The loving parent the child has known is gone, when an adult is taken over by rage. Once traumatized by abuse, she ceases to be the spirited, spontaneous, and emotionally responsive child or young woman she had been and becomes passive and obedient. This can also happen to a woman whose spouse terrifies her with his irrational and hostile fury. Adults who as children were the recipients of this kind of parental rage, to which alcoholism contributes, need to become aware of what happened to them as a beginning—and painful—step toward recovering an isolated, fearful, and depressed inner child, who is the key to becoming an authentically feeling person.

Imagine what it is like to be in a house with a powerful and angry figure who is a giant compared to you, just like an adult is to a child. There is no one to protect you, and there is no place to go. This figure is intoxicated with rage or alcohol and rage, his or her words are hurtful, and he wants you to feel bad. There is no reasoning with him. You fear that he may strike and hurt you. There is sexual tension in the air. What he threatens to do is terrifying, and you can imagine it happening. Maybe he carries out his threat. And worst of all, this is no stranger but a person who has taken care of you and loved you, which makes it a terrible betrayal and terribly confusing. You may block out these memories and go unconscious, which Brunnhilde did on her rock for twenty years. The recovery of these memories, though painful, holds the promise of the possibility of a return of feelings that have long been "asleep."

When Brunnhilde hears Siegfried's horn and joyfully anticipates his coming only to be confronted by a stranger, who finds her vulnerable and will take her and become her master, the horror of what Wotan has set her up for strikes home. Her long sleep and then her love for Siegfried have kept this at an emotional distance.

The parallel situation in ordinary life is abuse or marital rape by a husband who is no longer recognizable as the lover whom the wife fell in love with, or the husband who promised to honor and cherish her. She is likely to stay with him if it is a recapitulation of earlier childhood abuse, which then becomes a fate "decreed by her father." Brunnhilde's passive obedience to Gunther is that of the abused child.

Brunnhilde is taken out of this passive, benumbed state when she is introduced to Siegfried and Gutrune. Siegfried looks at her without recognition and is with the woman who will be his bride. Brunnhilde is confused and stunned. What is happening is at first beyond belief. Then she sees the ring on Siegfried's finger that was forcibly taken by the man she thought was Gunther, and she starts to put things together. When it becomes clear to her what Siegfried has done, she cries out her anguish at the betrayal, and there are clarity and focus in her angry accusations. For the first time since Wotan unleashed his wrath on her and took away her identity as a Valkyrie, the spirited Valkyrie she used to be is back. It is with the authority she had as a Valkyrie that she tears Siegfried's fingers off the spear on which he falsely swears and seizes it herself to vow that he must die.

With the help of her intellect, Brunnhilde puts the pieces of her confused emotional past together as she remembers what happened. It is not just that abuse and betrayal are painful, and so memories get blotted out or repressed. There is also a deep confusion that makes her doubt her own experience, which clouds matters. When Brunnhilde looks at Siegfried, and he does not recognize her she is initially stunned and confused, which has real-life parallels when others do not verify past experiences. At this moment, Siegfried is like a man who once seemed to be deeply in love with a woman and later does not acknowledge that there was anything special between them; she is then twice betrayed, with another woman and in memory. His lack of acknowledgment that she has any reason to be upset is a source of confusion; when there is no consensual reality, it makes her feel as if what really happened between them happened only in her mind. Besides feeling hurt and angry, this makes her feel crazy and confused.

Children in dysfunctional families have similar reasons to be confused. An abusive parent sobers up the next day, or the rage passes, or the molestation takes place at night in the darkness, and the next morning that parent looks at the child as if nothing has happened and there is no reason to be upset, and there is every expectation that the child have fun at the equivalent of Brunnhilde's celebration of her marriage. In many dysfunctional households, the other parent is not there for the child and does not protect her, and no one acknowledges that anything bad is going on. It is very confusing, which makes children repress as much of what happened as they can and mistrust how they feel and what they perceive. Distinguishing between a bad dream and reality is a developmental task that most children naturally learn. This is considerably more difficult under abusive circumstances.

The truth of the situation is what Brunnhilde first becomes clear about. This is also true for adult children on the way to recovering their authentic selves. The truth is not pleasant, and it brings out unpleasant feelings: first pain and anguish at the betrayal and loss, and then anger and fury. Brunnhilde's anger is so great that she wants

Siegfried dead. This plays into the hands of Hagen, who lives for vengeance and power. Psychologically, becoming like Hagen represents a major danger on the way to recovery, in which revenge and a desire for power so that one might never be a victim again takes over the personality.

OATHTAKING AS THE TEST OF TRUTH: IN A MAN'S WORLD, BRUNNHILDE IS DISBELIEVED

Brunnhilde accuses Siegfried of betraying her, which if true would also bring dishonor to Gunther and Gutrune. They and their vassals demand that Siegfried assure them that "all she says is a lie." To assure them, he must swear on a spearpoint, and vow that he is telling the truth. Once he does, he is believed. When Brunnhilde places her own hand on the same spearpoint, and repeats how Siegfried has broken every vow, she is discounted and patronized as an overly emotional woman who needs some rest to get over her rage.

Women who make charges against men are often treated similarly: in police reports of domestic violence where the man's version is believed. In court, when accusations of rape are dismissed because the man is believed. In Senate hearings to determine whether a man is fit to be a Supreme Court justice, Clarence Thomas would be confirmed after he strongly denied Anita Hill's accusations about his sexual harassment of her. Thomas (like Siegfried) made no effort to refute her specific charges; it was enough that he was righteously angry. In a man's world, a man's word holds more weight than a woman's, and if she persists and becomes upset at being disbelieved, she is further discounted for her emotionality.

SIEGFRIED'S DEATH: THE TRIUMPH OF VENGEANCE AND COWARDICE

Once the hunting party comes upon Siegfried, the three men are together. Hagen and Gunther sit on either side of Siegfried; the character of each man and circumstances shaped by them and by others have brought them here. Gunther is greatly troubled by his complicity in planning Siegfried's murder and his knowledge of what is in store. Gunther is not an evil man, only a weak one who can be influenced to participate in evil. He is troubled by it, but the weakness of character that made him go along with Hagen has taken him step by step to this moment. Hagen has no misgivings. He is a man whose psyche has been shaped for this moment. He is like an intelligent machine, programmed by Alberich to carry out orders coded into him years before, awaiting this opportunity. Siegfried is unaware.

Men whose characters are like those of Hagen and Gunther (and even men like Siegfried) often have dreams of having murdered someone, and in an analysis where they are finally being heard, they may dream of being caught. The dreams are statements, clues written in symbolic images, that tell us what happened in their childhood or adolescence. In response to what was done to them, they killed a part of themselves; they sacrificed it, and even if this was required by a parent, in their dreams they are the guilty party, for they did it. The victim may be a child representing the trusting, affectionate, playful, or creative part of the man; sometimes the victim is a woman, representing his anima and/or an actual relationship, which he abandoned; or it may be a man who represents the killed-off part of the dreamer; or the victim's identity is vague and unknown, a statement that violence was done, but it is not clear to what or to whom in the psyche.

Hagen hands Siegfried a drinking horn, casually telling him as he does so that it has been rumored that when birds sing Siegfried knows what they are saying. Indeed he can, Siegfried explains, but for a long time he has not heeded their song. To do so metaphorically, he would have had to pay attention to his intuition and listened for his own inner voice of wisdom. For all of us, solitude and introspection are required to hear truth from this source, and Siegfried has been caught up in the extroverted activities of his new life as the hero. A little later Siegfried comments that since women have sung their songs to him, he no longer cares for birdsong.

As he recounts his adventures, Siegfried does not give a thought to what the effect on Gunther and the Gibichung vassals might be when he tells of his "glorious bride," Brunnhilde. Gunther is dismayed and shamed by Siegfried, who is humiliating him and his sister in front of their vassals.

A moment later, however, Gunther grabs Siegfried's arm as if to pull him out of danger from Hagen's spear. Perhaps it is an involuntary gesture from the part of him that does not want to be part of this murder; maybe he makes a split-second conscious decision to save Siegfried. In either event, he acts too late.

THE DEATH OF THE HERO ARCHETYPE

The hero is an archetype that may be lived out during a stage in a man's life (and sometimes in a woman's) or called upon when we need to face something that we fear. It may be a fear of what the neighbors will think, a prohibition against going beyond our social class or being more successful than a father, a fear of poverty that inhibits risk taking, a fear of telling the truth about what we feel or of looking foolish or being vulnerable, of standing up for a person or a dream or standing up to an authority figure. Whatever parents feared doing, thinking, feeling, or being is passed on to the child, who will stay an adult child if he passively accepts whatever he is told to fear. These are all inhibitions in the way of being authentically ourselves. To overcome these fears, a person must think clearly, be decisive, and then act courageously, which taps into the hero archetype that is a potential in all of us.

Hagen and Gunther are adult children. Hagen is doing what his father told him to do. Gunther is going along with something he is too weak to oppose. Both men also

are motivated by greed for power themselves, which devalued, unloved people usually seek. In killing Siegfried, they
symbolically kill the hero archetype in themselves. (However, nothing in the psyche can be killed for sure and forever; all archetypes are potentials that are nurtured and
developed by family, culture, and circumstance, ignored
and undeveloped, or actively punished and repressed.
Potential archetypes may be repressed or suppressed and
thus "buried," but they are not dead and buried, even if
they are apparently killed over and over again. As archetypes, they may come to life, just as buried memories may
resurface, even decades later.)

Gunther vacillates between being an accomplice to
murder and saving Siegfried's life. While Gunther is a shal-
low and cowardly man, he is the sort of person who is
thought of as basically decent; he likes and admires Siegfried, does not want his sister to suffer, and wants people
to think well of him. At the last moment, Gunther seizes
Siegfried's arm, as if to pull him out of danger or warn him,
but it is too late for Siegfried and too late for Gunther's
own hero archetype to act.

The hero is an archetype or a potential part of everyone's psyche. It may be the ruling archetype for a phase of
life, or be a positive aspect of the psyche that can be called
upon when needed. However, when it takes over and
comes to dominate a man's personality, it limits him. Men
who identify with the hero archetype may live in the glory
of their past deeds, telling old "war stories" to anyone who

will listen, or they may have a need to repeatedly be the
hero, compulsively taking on high-risk challenges: this is
so for some mercenaries, policemen, surgeons, stunt men,
and even businessmen who repeatedly take risks.

THE TRUTH IS OUT

When Siegfried's body is brought back to the Gibichung
hall, Hagen tells Gutrune that he was slain by a ferocious
boar. Drawing from some inner knowledge, she says Siegfried was murdered and blames her "treacherous brother."
Gunther immediately names Hagen as the murderer,
which he readily acknowledges.

The truth is out: what Gutrune feels to be true she
states aloud to the person involved in front of others. She
breaks the cardinal rules of the dysfunctional family and
has the truth acknowledged, witnessed, and expanded.
While Hagen is the murderer, she correctly calls Gunther
treacherous; he betrayed her by going along with the plan
to murder Siegfried.

The next issue to be clarified is power. Hagen claims
the ring of the Nibelung, and Gunther makes a counter-
claim that it belongs to Gutrune (and through her, to him).
They fight over the ring and Hagen strikes Gunther dead
(just as Fafner killed his brother in *The Rhinegold*).

Psychologically, Gunther is that vacillating, decent but
weak man, the adult child who has paid too much attention
to caring what people think and too little to what he really
feels, who needs to ally himself with the hero archetype in

himself, but does not. Under Hagen's influence, Gunther has compromised the loyalties and feelings he did have and has gone along with evil. The decent but weak man becomes the accomplice, who is isolated from others he once cared about and compromised totally; eventually Gunther "is killed by Hagen" under these circumstances.

Hagen can be a bad influence in his outer life, a strong personality who dominates him, or Hagen can be an inner shadow figure, a hidden, negative, hostile part of a man that eventually can take over a man with a Gunther persona if circumstances keep turning against him. The once pleasant and sociable man who cared about appearances then turns into a withdrawn, depressed, and hostile Hagen, who keeps to himself.

Once Gunther is dead, Hagen reaches for the ring on Siegfried's hand. But he does not get the ring, for the dead hero's arm rises of its own accord in a threatening way, as it would have in life if Hagen had tried to take the ring from Siegfried. The ring belongs to the hero, and though he was slain, the power he had is not to be relinquished in this way. Siegfried had gotten possession of the ring by killing the dragon and listening to the woodbird; the ring was for him what he said it was, a symbol of this heroic deed, and a ring he once gave to Brunnhilde as a token of love. A hero's assassin may win fame and notoriety, but he cannot take power from the hero for his own use; the power of a hero comes from his deeds, which another person cannot claim or take from his body, as one might steal wealth or dictatorial power.

One last truth remains to be revealed. Gutrune considers herself Siegfried's widow, and as Brunnhilde comes forward, Gutrune accuses her of arousing men against him with her words. Brunnhilde responds gently, "Poor creature, peace! For you and he were not wed; you were his mistress, never his wife." Brunnhilde is compassionate and clear. Qualities the Valkyrie had that were temporarily lost to her have been restored.

When Brunnhilde tells Gutrune the truth, she recognizes it immediately, even though she had been holding onto another reality a moment before, just as she knows when Siegfried's body is brought in that he was murdered. Gutrune does not ask for proof, for when the truth comes, she knows.

This is an intuitive, feeling way of knowing, one that is often characterized as feminine intuition, because women seem to trust an inner gnosis or knowledge more than most men are willing to do or at least to acknowledge.

In dysfunctional families, people do not speak the truth about many or most feelings other than those that the particular family considers acceptable; how people feel about each other is often kept secret from themselves and each other. When feelings are finally voiced and we are ready to hear, however, we know it—as Gutrune does.

When Gutrune hears Brunnhilde's words, she not only knows that she is speaking the truth but also faces the truth of her own actions and is ashamed. However, she blames Hagen for suggesting she give Siegfried the potion that makes him forget Brunnhilde and fall in love with

her. In her way, Gutrune is as weak and thereby treacherous as she accuses Gunther of being. Both ultimately are
held responsible—by life—for listening to Hagen.

BRUNNHILDE'S EVOLUTION THROUGH SUFFERING

Brunnhilde has experienced the full range of human emotions and human suffering. She loves three generations of
men in her own family lineage. She sees firsthand and
emotionally feels the destructive results of Wotan's quest
for the ring of power, upon Siegmund, Siegfried, and
Wotan himself. When she calls upon Wotan to witness and
hear her, it is to tell him that Siegfried was forced to share
in Wotan's curse, which has doomed him.

Brunnhilde is the daughter of Erda, the wise, and
Wotan, who sought wisdom. When Wotan wakes Erda to
ask if the swiftly turning wheel can be stopped, the answer
is beyond her knowledge. She tells him he can learn the
answer from their daughter, Brunnhilde, who is both wise
and courageous.

Brunnhilde has the courage to act from her heart,
which has made her human. Wisdom comes later after
much suffering and pain. Her words to Wotan are, "That I
in grief might grow wise." Her statement brings to mind
the wisdom that I believe comes only through the experience of a descent into loss, betrayal, rage, and grief. Wisdom is the way out—what you find there, if you have the
courage to seek and face the truth—and it leads to opening

your heart again. Truth is about the reality of the situation and the character of those involved, including yourself. Wisdom draws from a deep human source and is accessible only after we let go of blame, guilt, and rage and can grieve.

Wisdom knows that all things will pass; that suffering is a part of life; that life is a meaningful spiritual journey; that renouncing love for power, wealth, and fame is a destructive choice based on fear; that love is the mystery we learn a little more about each time we risk pain by opening our heart to something or someone; and that change is inevitable.

Brunnhilde has evolved into a human who is both courageous and wise. As a daughter of Wotan and Erda, she carries two lineages in herself. She is a symbol of the person who can become free of patriarchy's obsessive need for power and yet have an authority, self-esteem, and capacity to act that being a Valkyrie—or a privileged daughter (or son) of the patriarchy—prepares a person for. Though Brunnhilde does not have a direct encounter with Erda, she has gone into the depths where grief takes a person and has found wisdom. The wisdom that comes from brooding upon suffering and grief and gaining knowledge with which one can go forward can be thought of as an encounter with Erda, who knows "what was, is, and will be."

As Brunnhilde contemplates Siegfried's body, whom she loved and to whom she has given all of herself and then hated with a murderous vengeance that contributed to his death, she knows that he was "the truest of lovers and most false," as she was to him. He had been the betrayer and the betrayed, and she had been also. She accepts what has been done and forgives. Looking at his face, she is like the mother or lover who gazes at her beloved's sleeping face, which in sleep is innocent and vulnerable; in that moment, there is only love.

In this moment of contemplation, she knows "what must be," and, guided by this inner certainty and wisdom that come from love, Brunnhilde knows that she must take the ring and wear it into the fire, where it will be cleansed of its curse, after which it can be returned to the Rhine. "Bequeathing only love!" she throws the torch onto the pyre. Then, calling her horse, she rides him into the fire.

Love itself is the pure gold that Brunnhilde bequeaths to us, the treasure that she came to know, through her humanity and wisdom. Power over others, which the ring of the Nibelung represents, is what we settle for only when we give up on being loved.

BRUNNHILDE'S FIERY END: SUICIDE OR TRANSFORMATION?

Brunnhilde rides Grane into Siegfried's funeral pyre, an act that sets them afire and signals Loge to ignite Valhalla, marking the end of the gods and the passing of the old order. She wears the ring of the Nibelung into the fire, bequeathing it to the Rhinemaidens after it goes through this fire of purification.

In real life, a woman who is betrayed and forgotten by the man she loves and in her pain and rage then provides the information that will destroy him might be filled with guilt. She might commit suicide under these circumstances. If she does, she will be literally doing something that does need to be done psychologically, which is true for people who contemplate suicide, in general.

The mistake is in doing literally what is called for symbolically. Suicide is an expression of the longing for the end of the pain of this life, an act of self-determination designed to set one free. Suicide often is also a ritual act of purification, an offering to cleanse a soul of guilt, of jealousy, of whatever seems too bad inside oneself to go on living with. It can also be a ritual act of expression, in which the intent is to deliver a message, a truth that the suicide mistakenly thinks will finally be heard. Or it can be intended as a means to bring about a union with someone who has already died, because one feels so incomplete alone.

The symbolic aims of suicide are freedom, purification, expression, and a longing for wholeness, which the suicide really wants to have in this life.

If anyone would follow Brunnhilde into the fire metaphorically, the task to be accomplished, as the alchemists knew, is to burn off the impurities and drive out the moisture in order to become pure whitened ash. Whatever shadow qualities cling to the soul, are the impurities to be burned away: vengefulness, anger, jealousy, pride, depression, despair, guilt, and shame.

Truth is the fire that destroys and purifies dysfunctional relationships, families, and institutions as well as freeing the individual. True feelings, remembered suffering, and acknowledged betrayal of the Self and others bring an end to all outmoded roles, old power structures, and destructively held secrets. Only then can the cycle of dysfunctional behavior stop.

Moisture as a metaphor stands for feeling and emotion, which are driven out by fire. The blazing pyre consumes the body, which is ninety seven percent water, metaphorically freeing the soul from the desires and cravings of the body, which may have held it in thrall to a person or an addictive substance. The pure ash that remains is the symbolic essence of a person, that which has come through the fire intact and true.

To get through the fire as an inner alchemical or transformative process takes psychological and spiritual work, twelve-step work, meditation, and work on and with one's body, whatever in itself and in combination exposes the soul to the fire that illuminates and destroys destructive patterns of being, burning away what needs to go, in order to free a person from compulsive behavior, destructive emotions, or addictions.

Brunnhilde tells the Rhinemaidens that after the fire has consumed the pyre, the river will rise and overflow the bank, taking the ashes and the ring of the Nibelung back into the Rhine. Now purified, the ring will become the Rhinegold once more—a source of beauty, purity, and numinosity in the depths of the river. The ashes of Brunnhilde and Siegfried—now mixed together—will be immersed in its waters. As an alchemical process, once we go through the fire, immersion in water follows: feelings return, and we are revived. Once again we are immersed in the river of life.

The Rhinegold is a symbol of the archetype of the Self that illuminates our depths. Once it is where it belongs, we no longer mistake this true gold, which is a spiritual power we cannot possess, with something that if we possessed it would give us power in the world. It frees us from a compulsive need to acquire power, fame, wealth, work, intoxicants, or addictive love as a substitute for a connection with the Self, through which we know that we matter and that love and beauty exist in us.

CHAPTER 5

Freeing Ourselves from the Ring Cycle

THERE IS A MESSAGE FOR US ALL IN *The Ring of the Nibelung* about the necessity of discovering the truth of the situation so that we stop playing a part in our own version of the *Ring* cycle unaware. Just as we respond to dreams, depending upon the degree of readiness or resistance to the truth that they symbolically express, so it is that our readiness to see parallels between the *Ring* cycle and real life in a patriarchal, dysfunctional society where the obsessive quest for power distorts personalities and relationships thus depends. There are degrees of insight ranging from intellectual to transformative. When we absorb the truth of a powerful dream or insight, it changes us and makes it impossible for us to continue as is, which is why we often resist and deny what we know to be true. For example, almost everyone can recall warding off the truth about a significant relationship or about the inner necessity to make a change until the truth was unavoidable.

We do this because truth often means that we will be leaving our familiar world or will be cast out of it. Thus we ward off acknowledging that something is meaningless, that love is gone, or that abuse is taking place, often as long as we can.

Love and passion for someone or something, a calling that feels like destiny, the positive insights or truth within us, may also be resisted, because it will put us in conflict with others' expectations or our own loyalties, because it will require that we sacrifice who we are now and how we are seen by others, or because we do not know what will happen to us or others if we alter our course. Consciousness as the awareness of truth brings choice with it. Even if we do nothing, once we see and feel the truth of a situation, we know that doing nothing is a choice and that silence is consent.

Throughout the *Ring of the Nibelung*, we are confronted with parallels to real life, to our particular real life, in the same way that our dreams inform us of what is true. If you want to know more about your personal connections with the *Ring* cycle, I suggest that you recall the scenes and characters that made a strong impression on you and ask yourself what or who do they remind you of. For example, it flashed in my mind that a charming man who was trying to impress me and involve me in a project was "a Gibichung," shorthand for noting the narcissism, shallowness, and opportunism that made him resemble Gunther and served to warn me to not get involved.

FREEING OURSELVES

You can also return to those sections in this book that comment on scenes or characters that affected you and note whether the commentary rings true for you. Most invaluable, however, are your personal associations and memories: where does your mind take you? What situations in your own life echo the tensions between characters in the *Ring?* For example, any woman who basked for any part of her life as a Brunnhilde, in her father's or a father figure's approval and then lost it, may recall the situation and now begin to understand what happened. Any man who sees himself and his father as a wrathful Wotan may feel grief and sorrow that his rages instilled fear in his children, once he remembers how frightened he was as a child. Truth leads the way. When we are willing to look and acknowledge what happened to us and what we did, freeing ourselves from a cycle of dysfunction becomes possible.

In his *Hero with a Thousand Faces,* Joseph Campbell wrote about the hero's journey, which begins with the call to adventure. By making the choice to heed the call, the hero ventures beyond his known world. The man or woman for whom this pattern is true is a hero-adventurer; the journey is a quest, like that of explorers who set out for Antarctica, darkest Africa, or unknown Tibet. This archetype often motivated the immigrant who sought a better life in America, as well as being a component in countless others who go to college or the big city with a dream to fulfill. At the beginning of the quest, the hero-adventurer is usually confident and unafraid and is either unaware or minimizes the possibility that loss, suffering, and sacrifice will be part of his or her journey.

In contrast, most people whom I see in my office are in their middle adult years. They embark on what turns out to be an individuation journey that requires them to face the truth and the truth of their feelings, and risk genuine communication, in order to live authentically. For many, the journey begins unheroically with abandonment or divorce, a business failure, a serious physical ailment or a life-endangering one, a psychological illness, or the acknowledgment that one has been living a lie, is a codependent, or has an addiction. The step beyond the known world into psychotherapy or analysis that begins this journey is taken as a conscious choice born out of pain and necessity rather than as a call to adventure. However, I might add that when the soul becomes engaged in the process, and a person taps into an inner source of meaning, life does become an adventure.

Brunnhilde's Moment of Truth

WHEN BRUNNHILDE CONTEMPLATES THE DEAD BODY OF Siegfried, we witness an inner drama, expressed through the music and then her words. Grief, anguish, compassion, and the truth come together. This is the turning point that determines the end of the *Ring* cycle and the ring of power. In this moment of truth, Brunnhilde realizes and accepts all that has happened. She knows who she is and what she must do. She understands that Siegfried was both "the most faithful and most faithless of lovers," as she—by participating in his murder—has been also. They both betrayed each other and the love they pledged to be faithful to eternally. She has projected shadow and hero onto him and seen herself as victim.

Brunnhilde had given Siegfried her horse, shield, and knowledge; he was to be the hero, she the woman who waits for her hero to return. She resembles many independent women who once supported themselves and were active in the world, who then seem to forget this part of themselves when they fall in love, marry, and become dependent. In giving Siegfried all her attributes as a Valkyrie, Brunnhilde had lost touch with these qualities in herself. Now, Siegfried the hero is dead and will not be returning to her, but the hero archetype is back, as part of herself, enabling Brunnhilde to act fearlessly and decisively to do what she perceives needs to be done. (Correspondingly, in forgetting Brunnhilde, Siegfried had lost touch with that part of himself that could be tender and faithful.)

In this moment of revelation, Brunnhilde knows that the ring of power that had set the cycle in motion has to be purified and returned to the Rhine. She accepts this as her destiny, knowing that she will have to face pain and death and go into the fire. By this act of immolation and sacrifice, Brunnhilde will bring an end to the era of the gods. Valhalla and Wotan will go up in flames, and a new era can begin.

Contemporary women and men are symbolically following Brunnhilde into the fire when they recognize the truth and decide to act on it, which leads them to go through the fire of emotional affect. Truth inflames emotions and passions, which can consume or purify. Once this begins, the relationship world as we know it may indeed go up in flames and bring down the old order. Revealing family secrets is like uncovering corruption in government. It may bring an end to an era and allow for a new and positive beginning, or the one who tells the truth may become a banished, punished scapegoat.

When we decide to act upon what we know is true for ourselves, we do what we do with an intention whose outcome we can hope for but not foresee.

Moments of Truth:
Personal Turning Points

THERE ARE INTERIOR TURNING POINTS IN EVERYONE'S life. I think of these as "moments of truth," moments when we now know something to be deeply true for us, the acceptance of which will change our life. It may be an inner revelation about what really matters to us, about who or what we love. It may be a moment of clarity in which we know that we are in a destructive or meaningless relationship and no longer can deceive ourselves about the situation. It can be a revelation about the nature of reality, or the reality of divinity, which causes a radical shift in our philosophical, religious, or even scientific perspective, after which we can never again perceive the world and our place in it as we once did. Or the moment of truth may shatter an illusion about someone else upon which we have built a life or an identity.

The truth we are confronted with can seem to be "out of the blue" and totally unexpected, though we may surmise later that it was something we must have known for a long time that finally broke through our denial or resistance. In a moment of truth, we may be presented with something so important that it can change our life and our personal world; literally, it can have life-or-death consequences.

This was true for a woman attorney, a law partner in a large firm, whose success in litigation was a result of her ability to seek and get what was best for her clients, to be their voice and advocate, whereas she was mute about her own marital unhappiness and unable to change the situation. Her husband was a generation older. He was also an attorney and an authoritarian personality whom she had married while quite young. He was father, mentor, and patriarchal husband to her. He decided not only what they or she would do, but also what she should feel. Since divorce was unthinkable due to her upbringing, to make the best of it required that she numb and deny her feelings, which she seemed to do quite well by focusing her thoughts and energy on her law practice. This was what her life was like when she discovered that she had a lump in her breast.

She reacted to the possibility that she had cancer unemotionally. With her lawyerly mind, she sought opinions on who to consult and made an appointment with the most highly regarded specialist. A biopsy was done, after which she was to go to the doctor's office to hear what she had, what the prognosis was, and what should be done. When the time came, she sat across the desk from her doctor, the foremost question in her mind being, "What should I do?" not "What do I have?" for she knew without being told that it was cancer. The doctor began to speak, and she did not hear a word he was saying. For the first and only time in her life, she was hearing a voice in her head. It said, "You must get a divorce." To which she responded, out loud, "I will!" which startled the doctor in midsentence.

There is an ineffable something that accompanies moments of truth, in which feeling, knowledge, and action to be taken fall into place. The clarity of the moment stops time. There is an interior hush, a cessation of movement, an intaking, that precedes action. The moment of truth illuminates the totality of the situation and includes what now must be done. It is also an experience of wholeness, as information that we have avoided or facets of ourselves we have repressed, denied, or projected upon someone else now come into consciousness.

Such was the case for this attorney, who told me that she knew that her cancer had developed because she had stayed in this marriage, that it was metaphorically killing her, and that the cancer made it literally possible that it would. She immediately began divorce proceedings, with an inner certainty that the effectiveness of the cancer treatment depended upon her getting divorced. As a litiga-

tor, she had become a Valkyrie warrior who went into battles for her law firm and her husband, just as Brunnhilde
had obeyed Wotan's commands. Now, for the first time,
she took up her own cause and acted decisively on her own
behalf.

No words accompanied another unexpected moment
of truth, which happened to a woman whose life exemplified suburban success. To all outward appearances, she
was a woman who had it all, big house, successful husband, two attractive children, junior league, country
clubs, an enviable life. She happened to glance at a stack of
just-delivered brochures, while the man she had stopped
by to chat with responded to a phone call, and found herself reading about an experimental Ph.D. program in transpersonal psychology. What began as a casual browse
turned into a profoundly life-changing moment of truth.

Unexpectedly, she was flooded with joy, which can
accompany moments of truth. When everything comes
together in such a moment, there is a clarity about who
one is and what one can be; it is a moment of transcendence, a sacred and joyful moment, a body and soul experience in which heart and body feel filled and full of joy, and
sometimes of light as well. While it lasts for only a
moment, time stands still for the revelation.

Until she held that brochure in her hand, she did not
know what it was she was seeking or how much she
yearned to lead a deeper, more spiritually rooted life in
which her intellectual development would also have a
place. In that moment of truth and clarity, she responded

with an interior "yes!" that she would unfalteringly live, in spite of ridicule and opposition from husband, family, and parents. This was an unaccredited degree program: it was called "flaky" and referred to with disparaging humor as "translucent psychology." Her father would disinherit her over it, her husband resent it. Her mother would be unfailingly critical of her and sorry for her poor husband for putting up with this, and her children were encouraged to see what she was doing in a bad light.

What comes with moments of truth gives us an inner sense of certainty and clarity. In such an experience we know we matter and that there are meaning and purpose in life. It is an epiphany, a high point of coherence. While this is often subjectively and momentarily wonderful, following your bliss (to use mythologist Joseph Campbell's well-known phrase), which is another way to describe what happens, also requires sacrifice of the now-outmoded life, and with the sacrifice usually comes suffering, for others as well as oneself depending upon the resistance and the price of making a change. To set out on a course of action, knowing it is deeply right for you to do but not knowing what the cost will be to yourself and others, requires courage.

Moments of truth that change the world occur in individuals who, in expressing their personal truth, speak for an idea whose time has come and, in so doing, seem to tap collectively held feelings that can no longer be contained or ever put back again.

FREEING OURSELVES

The moment of truth that began the civil rights movement of the 1960s occurred on a segregated bus in Mont-
gomery, Alabama, when Rosa Parks, a weary, middle-aged
black woman, got on the bus after a long day's work as a
domestic and sat down in the front of the bus because
there were no empty seats in the back. She not only sat in
a section forbidden to blacks; she also refused to move
when confronted by authority and was arrested. Demon-
strations followed, in which every participant had to
decide to risk putting his or her body on the line for racial
equality and freedom from oppression. It was moment-of-
truth time, when belief and action either came together or
did not. Rosa Parks's "no" turned out to be a momentous
act of civil disobedience, a private act that had public consequences because it tapped some deep well of justice and
courage in others, including Martin Luther King, Jr., who
was the minister of a prominent black church in Mont-
gomery. His leadership, vision, and eloquence were essential to the success of the civil rights movement; they
would lead to his assassination and his place in history.

The Protestant Reformation, which had even greater
historical consequences, began with a moment of truth in
another Martin Luther, who was Martin Luther King, Jr.'s,
namesake. Martin Luther was an Augustinian monk who
wanted to stay within the church that was his spiritual
home. He did not want to be a heretic, but he could not
deny the truth of what his church was doing and could no
longer remain silent. When he tacked the document that

addressed these abuses on the church door at Wittenburg, it would lead to his excommunication, which he might have predicted, and to the Reformation, which he could hardly have anticipated. His words, "Here I stand, I can do no other," are echoed in the actions taken by each person who is compelled to act with integrity once the truth is accepted.

Acts of Truth

THINKING ABOUT THE EXAMPLES OF HISTORICAL, mythological, and ordinary people, I am struck by those moments in which a person declares himself or herself, says something or does something that sets the course, not knowing what will happen next and often fearing the worst. It is not an act in which we are assured of the outcome: we do not know whether everything will turn out well or even that the sacrifice called for will make a difference, yet to not respond from the depth of the feelings we have about the rightness of that act would be to deny who we are at the soul level.

Uncertainty is the case at the end of *Twilight of the Gods:* Brunnhilde acts upon the truth that comes to her as she contemplates Siegfried's body, she immolates herself on the pyre, and we do not know if the curtain will ever rise on a resurrected or transformed Brunnhilde, or upon a new era.

FREEING OURSELVES

A common metaphor compares our actions at crucial moments to "stepping into the void." Authentic behavior begins with acts of truth; it may take us metaphorically into the void, into the fire, or onto the cross, and for a time after we do not know what the outcome will be.

Brunnhilde's decision to go into the fire reminded me of Jesus in the Garden of Gethsemane, accepting that he is to go to the cross. Later, his cry on the cross, "My God, my God, why hast Thou forsaken me?" makes the point that once his course was irrevocable, he felt abandoned to his suffering, which is when doubt and misgivings enter. When we decide to do what is true, or speak up about it, our efforts may be greeted with hostility, denigration, and efforts to humiliate us; we may feel ourselves being crucified, abandoned by others and even by the certainty that got us there. Once we have declared ourselves, we are no longer able to resume our former position or role; we cannot go back to who we were. In some situations, once we take the position we have, as far as others are concerned, we are dead.

Deborah Wright, a Presbyterian minister, impressed me with a sermon that focused on the Saturday of Easter week, a day and a concept I had never thought about before. On Friday the crucifixion takes place. On Saturday, we do not know that there will be a resurrection. So it is in life. Once we declare ourselves, we step beyond our known world into the void, into the fire, or onto the cross. We make an irrevocable break with the past and go into a period of uncertainty in between that is like Saturday after the crucifixion. Following the initial reaction to the ending of a marriage or career, a major shift in priorities, a new religious or sexual orientation, going public as a whistle blower about corruption or being the one who speaks up about abuse within a family or organization, we usually find ourselves in a "Saturday" phase. Our old life and old identity are dead, and we go for a time into the underworld or underground: not knowing whether this will be a tomb or a womb, a burial of all promise or the beginning of new life; not knowing whether this will be the end of us, or whether Sunday will come and with it resurrection and transformation.

I once read of a dream in an essay by Sonia Johnson that made a lasting impression on me because the dream was such a vivid and eloquent statement about choice, commitment to act, risks, and uncertainty of outcome. As I remember it:

The dreamer is trapped on the edge of the rooftop of a tall building, when she sees a rope swinging toward her. She knows that she can either stay where she is or grab the rope. She decides to grab the rope and swings in a wide arc away from the building. As the rope reaches the end of the arc, she sees another rope coming toward her and knows that she must let go of the one she is holding onto and grab this second one, which she does. Once more, she goes as far as this second rope can take her, and then she must once again let go in order to grab a third rope that is coming her way, which is where the dream ends.

FREEING OURSELVES

In this dream, the dreamer begins a risky journey by leaving a stable structure on which she feels trapped and makes a decision that takes her into the void. Each rope takes her only so far. Will another one come in time? Will she be able to let go once again of what she has in order to go on? Will she ever get to a safe and meaningful destination?

The dream may be reflecting what it is she is already doing and be saying that the "ropes" will continue to come, or it may be presenting her with how it will be if she takes the initial step and goes for the first rope. What the building and the ropes represent, the dreamer would have to delve into herself to know or intuit from her own life.

This is a dream to which many men and women in midlife who reach a plateau on which they feel trapped in meaningless roles or relationships can relate: they occupy positions that provide status, income, and power, which is what they were supposed to aspire to achieve, and they did succeed, even if their hearts were never in it. To have done this with their lives is to have been enmeshed in their own *Ring* cycle, making their lives an extension of a quest for power or position, including being a wife or husband, which was at some fundamental level not of their own choosing. At the point in their lives when they know this, a "rope" appears in the form of an opportunity to do something that they could love or to be with someone with whom a deeply personal, intimate relationship might be possible. What will one do when such a moment comes, with all the uncertainties inherent in such situations?

Moments of truth can be compelling when inner certainty and circumstance come together, when what you must do now is clear, and you find the courage or outrage that enables you to take that significant step. Until something happens that is "the last straw," the truth of the situation is warded off, minimized, denied, rationalized away, and the status quo is maintained. Emotional pain that would inform us often does not break through into consciousness because it is buried under something else: addictions to substances or activities, depression, pervasive unfocused or misfocused anxieties, chronic pain, or chronic medical conditions. When people arrive at a psychotherapist's office, a medical doctor's, or a twelve-step program, it is usually because a defense against acknowledging painful truths has gotten out of hand. Common vernacular describes this as the result of having "stuffed" feelings away only to have them resurface disguised as a psychological or medical symptom.

We learn to "stuff" our feelings because they are unwelcome. In childhood, if we were made to feel ashamed when we expressed our feelings or if they provoked others upon whom we were dependent to withdraw from or punish us, we learn to do this. At the very least, if no one was interested in what we felt, we may have never learned to discriminate, name, and express our feelings. We thus remain emotionally undeveloped, "feeling illiterates," unable to read our own emotional states or those of others. At the very worst, when terrifying rages or verbal, physical, or sexual abuse is unleashed upon children, by parents or

FREEING OURSELVES

caretakers upon whom they depend for survival, not only feelings but also often memories are buried through selective amnesia, dissociation, and even multiple personalities.

Sanctuary: Finding a Place Where Truth Can Be Spoken

WHEREVER POWER (RATHER THAN LOVE OR JUSTICE) IS the ruling principle in any relationship, family, organization, or country, it is not a safe place to have feelings and speak the truth. Only when one reaches a sanctuary and gradually feels what freedom means can truth emerge. The degree of oppression and punishment differs from relatively benign to rule by terror, but the psychology of the situation is the same: a police-state mentality results, in which there are numbing and denial of feelings, repression of memory for painful events, and loss of spontaneity, leading to depression and obsessive or addictive behaviors.

The child who lives in a dysfunctional family internalizes the rules, just like citizens of a police state do. Thought control, suppression of feeling, and behavior inhibition are enforced after a while from within the person; under such circumstances it is safer to not know what you really feel toward those in power, whether parents or authorities, lest you inadvertently reveal it and be punished. What you feel about anything is either irrelevant or punishable when you are controlled by someone in power who needs you to reflect well on them.

Ideally, a safe place psychologically is within a relationship or relationships in which you can be in touch with your thoughts, feelings, and sensations without being punished, judged, or abandoned for having them. It is a place where you can trust that you will not be lied to and will be free of exploitation, where the other does not feel superior at your expense, does not betray your confidences or intrude upon your boundaries. Anything that takes advantage of your vulnerability is exploitation. Sanctuary has a spiritual dimension, which comes about when those involved feel or know that there is something sacred in each of them, and is aware that there is a spiritual, soul-recognizing element present in the relationship. I think it important to know what constitutes a sanctuary relationship and to also know that we do manage, sometimes quite well, in imperfect but good enough situations once trust is established.

Numbed Feelings

WHEN IT IS SAFE, AND THERE IS ANOTHER PERSON OR people who care about what happened to you in the past and what you are feeling now, repressed feelings can emerge and traumatic events be remembered. Even then, it is not easy. Many people from severely dysfunctional families cannot remember events and do not even know that they cannot remember until someone asks or others are volunteering information, and suddenly it dawns: "I can't remember anything that happened before I was six, or nine, or . . . ," for example. Or, "I have no recollection at all of the fifth grade," or "the seventh grade." Or, "I can't remember what it was like when we lived with . . . "

Sometimes, a like situation brings back the repressed memory. An abusive situation in adulthood such as a mugging or rape unleashes nightmares and memories that go back to childhood events. Commonly, a woman who dutifully or against her wishes has intercourse, as Sieglinde did with Hunding, does so by "numbing out" and submitting, keeping both current feelings and past abuse out of consciousness. Then, when she falls in love and finds passion and tenderness in a sexual embrace, she—like Sieglinde—may find that this sexual awakening also awakens memories and with them bad dreams, torment, and conflict about her sexuality.

Sometimes, traumatic events can be remembered in the same way that facts are retained, but without emotion: "My mother drank too much. She would bring men home, sometimes more than one, and I would hear them having sex and see her passed out on the bed, naked, in the morning." Or, "My father used to hit my mother and beat up my brother, bad." Or events are described as normal that are not, again with apparently no feelings: "My father used to examine my vagina when I came home from a date"; "My mother and I slept in the same bed until I was in high school."

Siegfried was raised by the dwarf Mime, who lied to him and hated him, as a means of acquiring the ring of power. Siegfried became a man without feelings. Love was absent from Hagen's childhood as well. His sole purpose, for which Alberich bought a woman to conceive him, was also to help his father acquire the ring. To accomplish this, Hagen was taught to hate. Both Siegfried and Hagen could think, plan, and remember events as facts but did not feel. This is the fate of children who are used and abused by narcissistic parents or caretakers and grow up unaware of their own feelings. They learn to dissociate themselves from feelings for their own suffering and are contemptuous of the weak and without sympathy or empathy. They enjoy exercising power over others. When they are soldiers who are fearless warriors in battle, they are called heroes. When they commit crimes, they are called psychopaths. When they rule countries and are tyrants, they are called dictators. They do what they do without remorse. Usually the lack of feeling and ability to inflict pain on others reflect the brutality within the dysfunctional family in which they were raised.

Ordinary dysfunctional families are ones that repress feelings, or families in which a parent is an alcoholic. In these families, the ability to know what you feel and to express what you feel is discouraged. This accounts for emotionless reactions to present events that would otherwise evoke feelings. Hidden behind explanations, psychological analyses, and enlightened philosophical perspectives, one uncovers the truth, which is avoided: that is, "I don't feel anything."

FREEING OURSELVES

I have been struck with how widespread it is that people do not know how they feel much of the time. I see this as especially true for men, and increasingly so for women. More often than not, however, women do pay attention to what other people may be feeling. In any situation where someone has power over us, adaptation, survival, or success depends upon meeting their expectations, avoiding angering them, doing whatever is required to get into or stay in their "good graces." So it is that women who occupy dependent positions in society, as well as men who are in inferior positions because of their status or skin color, pay attention to the moods and character of those in power and of necessity may need to act deferentially and suppress whatever might be provocative.

Acting deferentially, which means suppressing our feelings and thoughts, is something we all do in the presence of power that could be used against us. For example, when the blinking light of a police car signals us to pull over to the side of a road, most people feel an adrenaline rush that is a "flight or fight" body reaction. We not only suppress the impulse to run in fear or express anger, we also usually act deferentially. This is an alarm reaction followed by adaptive behavior. It has the same effect as the raised, drunken, or angry voice of someone who has power to hurt or shame us. We fear the consequences of not responding as we are expected to and so learn to adapt by doing this rather than act on what we authentically feel. This is the basis of codependent behavior.

Ring of Power:
What Goes Around Comes Around

IN THE *RING OF THE NIBELUNG,* POWER OVER OTHERS IS the obsessive quest that affects three generations of Wotan's family, causing pain and suffering to all. Brought into existence by Alberich, who forges it by renouncing love, the ring is to be a ring of vengeance, with which Alberich will avenge himself for the humiliation and rejection he has suffered. Once the ring is in existence, it obsesses Wotan, not only because he wants it but also because if he does not have it, someone else can obtain it and have power over him.

Power over others serves psychologically as a means of obtaining a sense of security by having more power than others (which never really works: the saying "uneasy lies the head who wears the crown" is a testament to this). Psychologically, power over others is also sought in order to feel superior, a goal that compensates for underlying feelings of inferiority (which remain, however high the person goes up the ladder and takes on the trappings of success, and are responsible for widespread feelings of being "an impostor" in driven people who achieve status). Power over others is also exercised to ward off feeling little, insignificant, or weak and is responsible for the sadistic belittling behavior on the part of people with power.

The child is father to the man in the worst way when it comes to power; such a man grows up to become a tyrant, getting back for what was done to him. In his drive for power, he uses his children, making them, if he can, into extensions of his need for acquisition of power, prestige, and position in the world. In turn, unloved by him, his children work to please him, hoping that he might love them, or seek to be like him so as not to be insignificant as he makes them feel. Adult children from dysfunctional families ruled by contemporary Alberiches can become like Hagen, unrelated, power-seeking, angry men, or like Hagen's half-siblings, Gunther and Gutrune, whose adult achievements cover unhappy, unloved, scared, and angry inner children and whose choice of spouses and willingness to manipulate them into love-less marriages create the next generation of dysfunctional families. When power rather than love rules families, this *Ring* cycle continues through generations.

In the absence of love, as each generation ruled by power grows old, the insecurity of childhood returns with the dependency that age and infirmity bring. Sometimes, child abuse begets elder abuse, a terrible *Ring* cycle in which the abuse goes around in one generation, as the child who was abused becomes the abusing adult to the aged parent who abused him. To break this or any cycle of abuse, compassion must enter, and with it an acknowledgment of the suffering that was endured by all concerned.

Compassion for the Abandoned Child

A CHILD WHO IS NOT CARED FOR OR CARED ABOUT IS abandoned. Every adult in the *Ring of the Nibelung* whose childhood we know of was an emotionally abandoned child.

Wotan, the father of Siegmund, Mime, the caretaker of Siegfried, and Alberich, the father of Hagen, saw children as means of acquiring the ring of power, and whatever suffering they experienced as a result was inconsequential. Ambitious, narcissistic parents have children to further their own ambitions, enhance their image, reflect well on them, or carry on the family name. Children are abandoned emotionally when they are not loved for themselves, if their needs are unimportant, and it does not matter what they feel. Adult children can also be abandoned, as was Brunnhilde when she went against Wotan's will, and was shocked to learn that the loving father she thought she had planned to punish her by leaving her unconscious on a rock to be possessed by the first man who came along.

Children who are treated badly think of themselves as bad. Working with adults who have been abused as children, I see over and over again that there must be an innate sense of justice built into us. When children are abused, for example, their sense of justice makes them justify their treatment. They usually assume that they must deserve to be punished, either because they did something bad or because they are bad. When children are picked on and called dirty or stupid or a slut, they usually decide that this must be so. Children take the blame. They spare their parents and caretakers and adopt toward themselves the attitudes of those adults who abused them. The child then suffers from the double abuse of being badly treated and assuming that it is deserved.

This child remains a sad, abused, and abandoned inner figure, who is a source of low self-esteem and depression in the adult, who feels that "there is something loathsome about me" or "I'm a terrible person." When physical, emotional, verbal, or sexual abuse is uncovered, I hear stories that are heart wrenching. Yet even then, the adult who tells me what happened to him or to her in the past initially has no compassion for the child he or she was and is not outraged at the parent or caretaker who did what they did. Feelings of compassion for the maltreated child they used to be come slowly, and then only after someone else expresses them. There is a similar resistance to holding the abusive adult responsible. Abandoned and abused children are often protective of the adult who abused them. Not until they can feel compassion for themselves can they even be angry at what happened to them. Numbed feelings and forgotten memories are common in people who were abused or neglected as children, who often then go on to abuse or neglect their own children in similar ways. Or they go on to be codependents, taking care of and rationalizing the behavior of people who abuse them, like they did their parents. Deference to power is at bottom a learned dynamic, which passes through the generations.

When children are abandoned emotionally, they grow up to be unhappy adults who ward off feelings of emptiness, abandonment, sadness, rage, impotency, shame, and other distressing feelings by drinking, smoking, eating, watching television, and behaving in all sorts of compulsive ways.

Addictions, codependency, and depression keep us from feeling our emotions and recognizing our visceral sensations, which could inform us of the truth of our situation.

Freed from the *Ring* Cycle

ONLY WHEN WE CAN FEEL OUR FEELINGS AND RECOGNIZE why we have them can we know what gives our lives meaning, what kind of work or what relationships matter to us personally. It is necessary for us to become conscious of our feelings before we can make authentic choices based on love of place, work, and persons, or for spontaneity and joy to be part of our lives. In order for us to know what we feel, significant others have had to care about us and been concerned about how we feel. It has had to be or become safe for us to speak the truth and to act upon what we know. Once we can act upon what is true for us, our choices shape our lives, and our lives are expressions of what genuinely matters to us (provided, of course, that we have the freedom to choose and opportunities to choose from). Only then are we free of the ring of power.

CHAPTER 6

Beyond Valhalla:
A Postpatriarchal World?

WHEN THE CURTAIN COMES DOWN ON THE *RING* CYCLE at the end of *Twilight of the Gods*, Valhalla, Wotan's fortress-castle, has just gone up in flames. Inside the vast hall, with branches of the world ash tree stacked against its walls like firewood, Wotan awaits the end, seated among heroes who had died on battlefields, Valkyries, and deities. When flames from Brunnhilde and Siegfried's pyre reach Valhalla and ignite the conflagration, the sky lights up like a fiery, dramatic sunset, heralding the end of Wotan's waning supremacy. Like a curtain, night will fall on the smoldering ashes of Valhalla and the passing of an era of patriarchy obsessed by the ring of power. While Valhalla is burning, the ring of the Nibelung is reclaimed by the Rhinemaidens, as Brunnhilde intended, and is returned to the depths of the Rhine. The coveted ring, with which one could rule the world, will no longer be in the world, and a new era can begin. Dawn will come, and we are left wondering, on what?

A postpatriarchal world would indeed be a new age. I speculate on the possibility that we are in a historical period that corresponds to a twilight of the patriarchy and an archetypal time of major transition. There are signs of such a possibility. With nuclear weaponry, the power to rule the world cannot be separated from the power to destroy the planet. If this were to truly sink in, and the necessity to affiliate rather than dominate became the new priority—across the board, in all relationships and institutions—it would be the end of the patriarchy.

Visible in political systems worldwide is a growing disrespect for the authority of old men, and regimes they head are falling. Psychologically, the archetype of the distant, power-oriented authoritarian father is losing psychic energy. A new planetary consciousness with strong ecological concerns is emerging. Feminism made us conscious of patriarchy and its negative, repressive effects on women. With its power orientation and emphasis on domination and hierarchy, the patriarchy is increasingly viewed as destructive to men and to the planet as well.

A Time of Transition

IN HUMAN PSYCHES EVERYWHERE, THERE IS AN ANTICI-pation of change. We are on the edge of a new millennium, as the years 2000 and 2001 approach. There is something in the collective unconscious that responds to this major symbolic date. Like New Year's Eve, a major birthday, or a special anniversary, there are dates that have significance in our psyches and thus an influence and power to affect us. Psychiatrists know to ask about "anniversary reactions," for example, that often make sense of the timing of an otherwise inexplicable mood or act. Psychologically, when we anticipate the possibility of a new age or new beginning, we are ourselves open to change, and this very anticipation contributes to making change likely.

We are also in the midst of a transition period or cusp between two astrological ages: a two-thousand-year Piscean age is passing, and we are moving into the age of Aquarius at the same time as we move into a new millennium. The Piscean age (or age of the fishes) corresponds to the patriarchal Christian era. The fish symbol was used by early Christians to identify themselves to one another, because *Ichthys*, the Greek word for fish, was an acronym for "Jesus Christ, Son of God," words that were mockingly put upon the cross on which he was crucified. It is a synchronicity that the age of Pisces would turn out to be defined by this event, from which the fish became the symbol.

This is also a major time of transition in Hindu mythology, which has five-thousand-year cycles. Each cycle begins with a golden age, which subsequently deteriorates into the silver, copper, and iron ages. According to this tradition we are in the lowest, most debased period, the iron age, and will have to pass through a time of destruction or deconstruction before a new golden age can begin.

I was introduced to this Hindu concept in India by the Brahma Kumaris Sisters, who follow a Raj Yoga tradition.

Believing we are indeed at the end of the iron age, but believing that people can affect the quality of the passage that will inevitably come, they work through the United Nations and throughout the world, as I see it, on the spiritual underpinnings of peace. Through one program, people pledged millions of minutes of meditation for planetary peace; through another, children and adults met in small groups all over the world to share their hopes and envision ways of making this a better world through cooperative efforts. If the manifest world of visible action comes out of the invisible world of thought, intent, and vision (in psychological terms, from the collective unconscious or morphic field or collective consciousness of humanity), these efforts would counter the pervasiveness of fear and the need for power that fear creates.

The Authoritarian Father Archetype

IN THE CULTURE, AS IN THE PSYCHE, AN ARCHETYPE CAN come to dominate an age in much the same way that an archetype can dominate or take over a personality. This has been so for the authoritarian father archetype in patriarchies. The authoritarian father is institutionalized atop every hierarchy; he is called by many titles, including king, pope, general, chief executive officer, president, and father, and his qualities are modeled upon those of the father god of that particular culture.

BEYOND VALHALLA

When a man occupies a position defined by this arche-type, he may identify with it, in which case he will act, think, speak, and behave as if he were the same as the archetype. Power over others changes people. It is not at all uncommon, for example, for some men to drastically change their personalities: when they are in a lesser posi-tion, they can be subservient, even fawning, toward a superior; when they are the ones with power, they can be dictatorial, impatient, and imperious toward those under them. They become petty tyrants, unsoftened by human qualities of humor, perspective, and individuality.

A man who identifies with the authoritarian father archetype may be a feared and hated dictator or be a beloved and respected father. In either case, authority over the oth-ers in his household or sphere and having the final word are assumed to belong to him. The authoritarian father arche-type, colored by experience with one's own father or father figures, lives in everyone. While males with power over oth-ers may personify the archetype, it also is experienced by many as an inner voice of authority who makes us feel small and insignificant. It is the fault-finding inner critic of our work as "not good enough," whose inhibitory "Who do you think you are?" keeps us from our aspirations.

This archetype stifles creativity, expression of feelings, playfulness, passion, and spontaneity in whomever it has an influence, because being in control would have to be given up in order to be open to these experiences — and being in control is essential to this archetype. The authoritarian father archetype has the most influence in patriarchal cultures. It gives the father authority over family members in families and has an inhibitory influence in the psyches of individuals. It will remain so unless egalitarian qualities such as truth and freedom or compassion and wisdom become more important than power. As long as patriarchy exists, whoever has the most power has the last word. Consequently, the authoritarian father archetype will stay pre-eminent, and power over others will be an obsession.

The gradual loosening of the hold of this archetype is chronicled in the *Ring of the Nibelung* through the changes we witness in Wotan. In *The Rhinegold* and *The Valkyrie*, Wotan is a self-centered, narcissistic, authoritarian father figure. He offers Freya to the giants in exchange for building Valhalla, unleashes his fury on Brunnhilde for disobedience, and abandons his Walsung children. He is an example of a man initially possessed by the archetype, whose quest for the ring of power causes himself and others suffering, and whose ambitions are frustrated by limitations on his power. In *Siegfried*, Wotan has changed. He has a more humble appearance. He is seeking wisdom and answers to questions and is conflicted over giving up or holding onto the power he has.

Wotan is like many contemporary men, who are obsessed with acquisition of power and possessions, sacrificing relationships as they do so, only to find at midlife or toward the end of their life that their power is waning and that what power remains is empty of meaning. Wotan was able to see that this was so, yet was unable to change. Thus, in *Twilight of the Gods*, Wotan awaits the end in Valhalla—as men do who remain identified with the authoritarian father archetype—depressed, distant, and surrounded by what he has acquired.

Wotan becomes the Wanderer after his quest for power leads him to experience his limitations and brings about suffering. As the Wanderer, he no longer is totally identified with the authoritarian father. He is in a period of searching, without a definite path, direction, or destination, as the very name Wanderer implies. This is that time of questioning and soul searching that comes to people at midlife and is a time when change may occur. In men, it is a transition time when the quest for power may be given up if they listen to their anima or inner feminine.

Thus Wotan summons Erda, feminine wisdom, to awaken and come to him, which she does. But because he had overpowered her earlier, Erda's clarity is no longer available. Her thoughts are "beclouded by the deeds of men"; her wisdom "had felt a conqueror's force." She tells him that their valiant and wise daughter, Brunnhilde, can provide the answers he seeks—and we know that this will not be possible, because he has banished her from him. Brunnhilde, symbolizing his compassionate feminine aspect, his anima, in Jungian terms, which would choose love over power, is asleep—unconscious, unavailable, repressed. Psychologically, we can say that Wotan cannot change because he has cut himself off from his anima.

In the psyches of individual men, however, a period of being the Wanderer can lead to major change. Acquisition of power can become secondary to relationships, if these men listen to their anima and value feminine wisdom. Relationships become more important. Marriages often go through a crisis time, and either more depth or divorce may result. Maintaining the form is no longer sufficient. Families and friendships take on new value. This is a time described by psychologist Erik Erikson, who provides us insight into the psychological challenges of each phase of life, when generativity occurs or stagnation sets in. Men may start a second family and this time spend time being a father, or they may mentor younger people. It is a time when emotional intimacy becomes possible if formerly authoritarian men are willing to be vulnerable. Love can become more important than power as a consequence.

Power can also reassert itself in the psyche of a man who is threatened by the emergence of feelings and thus represses them, just as authoritarian men who head patriarchal governments react to free expression of feelings by their citizens. They become threatened by the potential of change, of loss of authority, and clamp down. This happened in China's Tiananmen Square to students whose symbol was the Goddess of Liberty.

Enantiodromia or Evolution? Emergence of the Repressed Feminine

THE CONCEPT OF "ENANTIODROMIA" IS REFERRED TO often in Jung's writings. It refers to the flipflop that happens in the psyche when what has been held down suddenly gains the upper hand, as can happen in arm wrestling. To keep an arm pinned down takes muscle and exertion; similarly, keeping a lid on truth or suppressing an idea, an instinct, or an archetype takes psychic energy. For several thousands of years, since Indo-European warrior tribes with sky gods over-came goddess-worshipping peaceful people in old Europe, Western patriarchy has actively kept feminine values and authority, goddesses and women, "in their place," which is to say that whatever is considered feminine has been dom-inated, denigrated, denied, and actively held down.

In the psyche, an enantiodromia overcomes a one-sided psychological attitude. According to Jung, it is an expres-sion of the tendency toward wholeness, as what has been denied pushes toward consciousness. When it emerges, either it can be integrated into the personality, which becomes larger as a result, or a flipflop occurs, and what was on top now is on the bottom.

We have become aware, through the writings of Marija Gimbutas, Merlin Stone, Riane Eisler, and others, of a prepatriarchal time when peaceful, goddess-worshipping people inhabited old Europe. Even though this information did not come to us until the middle to late twentieth cen-tury, mythology remembered these times. Storytellers and artists have tapped into these images and themes, which are in the collective unconscious. Thus we now find that the recitation of events by the Norns at the begin-ning of *Twilight of the Gods* is a remarkably accurate reflection of these events told in metaphor.

The Norn story begins with the world ash tree, whose green shade shelters a spring in which wisdom's voice can be heard. It is a time when humans are part of nature and can tap into the wisdom of the earth. Like the tree whose branches reach high into the sky and whose roots reach down into the earth, the mental and the physical realms come together; the underworld and the upper world are of equal importance.

The world ash tree is a symbol of the Self, the archetype of wholeness. The Self is what people feel close to when they are at home in the wilderness and share a world view with the Native American, related to Father Sky, Mother Earth, and all life. When ego is related to the self, we feel whole and in harmony with the world, with nature, with the Tao. It's also what we experienced in our dimly recalled personal past, when we were one with our mother.

Trees and springs were sacred to the goddess and to the Druid. Thus the world ash tree and the spring also are symbols of the goddess. Sacred sites had churches built over them in the British Isles and Europe. The people who worshipped there were persecuted and reviled as pagans and heathens by Christians. *Pagan* comes from the Latin *pagani*, which means "country-dwellers." *Heathen* comes from the German *heiden*, "that which is hidden." Once worship of the goddess was forbidden, pagan rites had to become secret.

As a symbol of wisdom, the spring brings clear, pure water from underground sources. Water is necessary for life; it makes growing things green. As a metaphor, wisdom from a spring that arises from the earth is different from that which comes from the mind, in words or as abstract concepts. Wisdom from the earth is wisdom that comes from the body, wisdom that comes from life. Feminine wisdom is grounded in nature, in being in a body that is a vessel for life. This is a wisdom that affirms the sacredness of the physical world.

Returning to consciousness at this transition time is a growing awareness of feminine wisdom and its repression, a memory kept alive in mythologies that describe the disappearance of the goddess of wisdom. In the *Ring of the Nibelung*, which was inspired by Teutonic/Norse mythology, Erda disappears into the earth to sleep. In Greek mythology, the prepatriarchal goddess of wisdom is Metis, who is tricked into becoming small and swallowed by Zeus. Through the *Nag Hammadi* scrolls, which were uncovered in the Sinai desert in the midtwentieth century, we learned that the gnostic Christians believed in a feminine wisdom aspect of divinity that they called Sophia. Persecuted as heretics, what remained of their beliefs in Wisdom/Sophia were literally buried until now and are well described in Elaine Pagel's *The Gnostic Gospels*.

The Norns explain what happened to the world ash tree and the spring as an inadvertent consequence of Wotan's acts. Wotan drank from the spring and broke a branch from the tree to make the spear with which he would rule the world. He carved his laws and agreements into the shaft of the spear. After that, as year succeeded year, the tree slowly died, and the spring stopped flowing. Finally, the time came when Wotan ordered the tree hacked down, and the wood was heaped against the walls of Valhalla. Just as the death of the tree and the drying up of the spring marked the end of the time of the goddess, when Valhalla burned, it would mark the passing of Wotan's age, the end of patriarchy.

Culture can behave like an individual psyche. If an enantiodromia occurs, what was repressed now takes over the personality. The sinner becomes the saint, and vice versa, for example. The cultural equivalent is a political revolution in which power shifts, like a pendulum from one pole to the other.

Culture can also behave like a healthy, open, and flexible personality that accommodates and assimilates new information, events, people, feelings, and thoughts, so that consciousness can expand and grow (though not without resistance to change). Times of transition are bumpy times, filled with ambivalence, dissatisfaction, uncertainty of direction, moments of truth, and decisions to make. This is so for institutions, organizations, and businesses as well as for cultures and individuals.

At midlife, especially, interior unrest occurs, through which the personality either opens up to change or shuts down and becomes more set in its ways. Men who have identified with the authoritarian father archetype or conformed to expectations of a patriarchal culture that they compete for power and achievement (as women are also increasingly doing) find themselves in a transition phase, not unlike where Western patriarchy finds itself.

BEYOND VALHALLA

Men separate from the mother realm or feminine sphere when they enter the patriarchal world of school and work. Repression and devaluation of the feminine follow, just as knowledge of the goddess and knowledge of a matriarchal time were forgotten or denied, historically. Paralleling the threat to the status quo at midlife, which happens to individuals when the repressed feminine aspect of the personality or anima makes its influence known, the repressed feminine is emerging into patriarchal culture in its many forms of expression. All have to do with relationship and interdependency.

Beyond Valhalla: As a Postpatriarchal Personal Dimension

WHEN *THE TWILIGHT OF THE GODS* ENDS, ONLY THE ashes of the funeral pyre and Valhalla remain. It could be a depressing ending, yet it is not. Just as hope springs eternal in the human breast, as the phoenix arises from the ashes, as Hiroshima and Nagasaki arose from the rubble of the atomic bomb, there is something in us that responds to the end of the *Ring of the Nibelung,* knowing that a new era is now possible, when Valhalla is no more and the ring of the Nibelung is returned to the Rhine. As an enactment of an interior drama, the *Ring* cycle is alive in all of our psyches. The patriarchy has a powerful hold on our inner lives, as power dominates the outer world in which we live. Whether Valhalla disappears and the ring of power is redeemed by the Self, each of us has to decide for ourselves, if we can.

Brunnhilde's example tells us what we can learn from life. When we go through suffering, accept our own shadow instead of projecting it onto others, face the truth with compassion, and have the courage to act with integrity, our defenses and denials drop away and we can see clearly and know what truly matters. We then find that possessing someone or something, gaining power over others, becoming famous now or in the hereafter, or getting revenge, are no longer compelling goals. Only then are we likely to discover that there is indeed a source of wisdom and healing in our depths, which is the pure gold of the psyche, love.

The Ring of the Nibelung

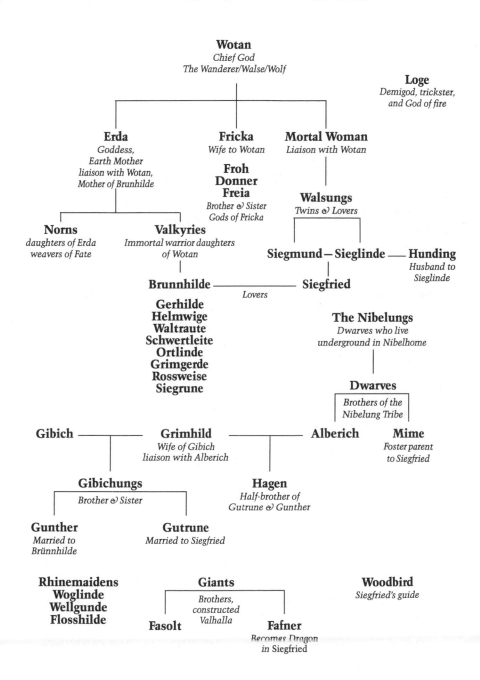

Wotan
Chief God
The Wanderer/Walse/Wolf

Loge
Demigod, trickster,
and God of fire

Erda
Goddess,
Earth Mother
liaison with Wotan,
Mother of Brunhilde

Fricka
Wife to Wotan

Mortal Woman
Liaison with Wotan

Froh
Donner
Freia
Brother & Sister
Gods of Fricka

Walsungs
Twins & Lovers

Norns
daughters of Erda
weavers of Fate

Valkyries
Immortal warrior daughters
of Wotan

Siegmund — Sieglinde —— Hunding
Husband to
Sieglinde

Brunnhilde ——————— Siegfried
Lovers

Gerhilde
Helmwige
Waltraute
Schwertleite
Ortlinde
Grimgerde
Rossweise
Siegrune

The Nibelungs
Dwarves who live
underground in Nibelhome

Dwarves
Brothers of the
Nibelung Tribe

Gibich —————— Grimhild ————— Alberich
Wife of Gibich
liaison with Alberich

Mime
Foster parent
to Siegfried

Gibichungs
Brother & Sister

Hagen
Half-brother of
Gutrune & Gunther

Gunther
Married to
Brünnhilde

Gutrune
Married to Siegfried

Rhinemaidens
Woglinde
Wellgunde
Flosshilde

Giants
Brothers,
constructed
Valhalla

Fasolt

Fafner
Becomes Dragon
in Siegfried

Woodbird
Siegfried's guide

GLOSSARY

CHARACTERS, CREATURES, OBJECTS, AND PLACES

ALBERICH: the Nibelung dwarf who forges the ring of the Nibelung, has it taken from him by force, and is obsessed with repossessing it; father of Hagen

BRUNNHILDE: the Valkyrie, virgin immortal warrior daughter of Wotan and Erde, who disobeys Wotan and is punished by losing her immortality and her virginity to Siegfried

DONNER: god of thunder and lightning, which he can evoke with his magic hammer; protective brother of Freia

DRAGON: once Fafner the giant, who changed himself into a dragon in order to guard his treasure, which included the ring of the Nibelung and the Tarnhelm; killed by Siegmund with his sword, Notung

ERDA: goddess of wisdom, who resides deep in the earth, an earth mother whose influence precedes Wotan's; mother of Brunnhilde

FAFNER: a giant who becomes a dragon; one of two brothers who are the last of a race of giants and master builders who build Valhalla. Fafner kills his brother Fasolt to obtain the ring of the Nibelung and uses the Tarnhelm to transform himself into a dragon to guard his treasure.

FASOLT: a giant and master builder, who with his brother Fafner builds Valhalla; killed by Fafner

GLOSSARY

FREIA: goddess of youth, love, and beauty, who cultivates the golden apples that the deities must eat to retain their youthful immortality; sister of Fricka, Froh, and Donner; promised by Wotan to the giants as payment for building Valhalla

FRICKA: Wotan's wife, goddess of marriage and fidelity, sister of Freia, Froh, and Donner

FROH: god of the fields, protective brother of Freia, who created the Rainbow Bridge to Valhalla

GIANTS: two brothers—Fafner and Fasolt—the last of their race of master builders who built Valhalla

GIBICHUNGS: Gunther and Gutrune, descendants of Gibich, who were an ambitious brother and sister

GOLDEN APPLES: the magic apples cultivated by the goddess Freia. Eating them daily kept the divinities from growing old.

GUNTHER: a Gibichung mortal, ruler of a fiefdom on the Rhine, son of Gibich and Grimhild, brother of Gutrune, and half-brother to Hagen through their mother

GUTRUNE: a Gibichung mortal, sister of Gunther, half-sister of Hagen; marries Siegfried after giving him a potion that causes him to forget Brunnhilde and desire her

HAGEN: the illegitimate son of Alberich the Nibelung and Grimhild, half-brother to Gunther and Gutrune who kills Siegfried

HUNDING: Sieglinde's husband who kills Siegmund with Wotan's help

LOGE: trickster demigod and god of fire. In *The Rhinegold* he is a quick-thinking trickster figure, who travels widely and gathers information; in the operas that follow, his identity as god of fire is the more important.

GLOSSARY

MIME: a Nibelung dwarf and Alberich's bullied brother who makes the Tarnhelm; foster parent to Siegfried

NIBELHOME: underground home of the Nibelung dwarves

NIBELUNGS: dark dwarves who live underground (in Nibelhome), who mine gold, work at forges, and are craftsmen

NORNS: three daughters of Erda, the goddess of wisdom, who weave the cord of destiny that determines fate

NOTUNG: "Needful," the sword Wotan promises that his son Siegmund will find in his hour of need, that Wotan buries up to its hilt in the tree in Hunding's house. Shattered by Wotan's spear, and reforged by Siegfried, it is used to kill Fafner the dragon.

RAINBOW BRIDGE: a rainbow and a bridge created by the god Froh over which the deities cross to Valhalla

RAVEN: Wotan's bird, which announces Wotan's presence or carries news to him

RHINEGOLD: the magic gold that was in the depths of the Rhine river until Alberich stole it and forged the ring of the Nibelung from it

RHINEMAIDENS: three river nymphs whose task it is to guard the Rhinegold: Flosshilde, Wellgunde, and Woglinde. They divulge the secret of forging a ring of power from the Rhinegold to Alberich.

RING OF THE NIBELUNG: the ring of power with which one can rule the world; forged by Alberich the dwarf, who renounces love in order to make it, hoarded by Fafner the dragon, who comes to possess it, won by Siegfried, who gives it to Brunnhilde as a token of love; coveted by others

GLOSSARY

SIEGFRIED: the hero who has no fear; son of Siegmund and Sieglinde, the twins fathered by Wotan, who was orphaned at birth and raised by Mime, his foster parent, who kept him ignorant of his parentage

SIEGLINDE: wife of Hunding, daughter of Wotan and a mortal woman; Siegmund's twin sister who becomes his lover; mother of Siegfried

SIEGMUND: referred to as "the Walsung." His father is Wotan, who as "Walse" mates with a human woman and creates a new race, called the Walsungs. Father of Siegfried, brother and lover of Sieglinde

SPEAR: see *Wotan's spear.*

TARNHELM: crafted by Mime the dwarf, imbued with magical powers by Alberich's use of the ring of the Nibelung. Whoever possessed it could take on any form or transport himself to any place.

VALHALLA: castle-fortress envisioned by Wotan and built by the giants, home of the immortal deities and the heroes who die on the battlefield and are brought there by the Valkyries

VALKYRIES: nine immortal daughters of Wotan who ride their magic horses through the stormclouds of war, wear armor, and bring dead heroes who fall in battle to Valhalla: Brunnhilde, Waltraute, Gerhilde, Ortlinde, Schwertleite, Helmwige, Siegrune, Grimgerde, Rossweise

WALSE: Wotan's identity when he lives with a mortal woman and fathers the Walsungs, Siegmund and Sieglinde

WALTRAUTE: the Valkyrie who tries to persuade Brunnhilde to give up the ring of the Nibelung that Siegfried has given her as a token of his love

GLOSSARY

WANDERER: Wotan's identity when he is disguised as an old man in a broad-brimmed hat that covers his blind eye

WOODBIRD: Siegfried's informant and guide

WORLD ASH TREE: once the center of the world when Erda's dreams were woven into reality by the Norns. Wotan broke a branch off the tree to make his spear with which he ruled, after which the tree died. In *Twilight of the Gods*, it is cut into cordwood and stacked around Valhalla to await the conflagration that will bring Wotan's rule to an end.

WOTAN: the chief and most powerful god, who rules through agreements and treaties carved on his spear. He has one sighted eye, wears a patch over his other, and carries the spear. Known as Odin in Norse mythology, he is a sky god who rules from Valhalla; equivalent to the Greek god Zeus. Father of Brunnhilde, Siegmund, and Sieglinde when he lives with a human woman as Walse; as Wolf and Wolfcub, Wotan and Siegmund roam and hunt together for a time; as the Wanderer, Wotan appears as an old man with a broad-brimmed hat that covers his blind eye.

WOTAN'S SPEAR: symbol of Wotan's rule, made by him from a branch of the world ash tree. Agreements are carved into its shaft. Carried as a staff by Wotan in his guise as the Wanderer. Broken by Siegfried by a blow from his sword when Wotan attempts to bar his way to the mountaintop, where Brunnhilde lies asleep surrounded by the ring of fire.

In *The Rhinegold* and throughout the *Ring* cycle, location is always significant. I find it makes psychological sense to respond to where the scene is taking place as if it were a dream landscape and to interpret it accordingly. In the *Ring* cycle, scenes take place underwater, in the mountains, underground, and on land, and each location is metaphorically the appropriate place.

THE UNDERWATER REALM

The opening scene of *The Rhinegold* takes place underwater. Here the Rhinemaidens are at home, and Alberich is out of his element. The fluidity and murkiness of watery depths represents the unconscious realm of emotion, feelings, and instincts. Like the sea, any underwater world is often thought of as feminine, with the power to pull masculine mental focus into a dangerous realm, where one can be flooded by instinct or drowned in emotion and be made to feel foolish or be painfully rejected.

Consciousness, like sunlight, can penetrate the more surface depths of personal feelings and illuminate what is there. Going deeper, much that is either personal or collective may remain hidden or dark.

THE MOUNTAINS

A high place in the mountains is the site where we first meet Wotan. Here the other immortals are also present, and here

Erda comes to warn Wotan. All of the scenes with the Valkyries take place in the mountains. This is where Fricka comes to make demands upon Wotan. Erda is summoned in a mountain cave to meet Wotan. Soaring into the sky, mountains stand above the plane of ordinary existence.

Sky gods who rule from above, for whom law and will are paramount, always reside or meet humans on mountaintops. For example, Zeus ruled from Mount Olympus, which was the home of the Greek immortals, and Jehovah gave Moses the Ten Commandments on Mount Sinai. The mountaintop as a symbolic location represents the mental realm of the mind and the religious realm of transcendence with its emphasis on the spirit. When we go skyward spiritually, we rise above the body, emotions, and ordinary life.

When the emphasis of a religion or a culture is transcendence and hierarchical, the mountain is a liminal place, a place that lies between the ordinary world below and the vast sky above, where the human and divine worlds overlap or meet. In the *Ring of the Nibelung*, the mountain summit is the natural habitat for the immortals.

Psychologically, in all Western civilizations derived from Greece, the summit is the realm where culturally sanctioned archetypes dwell—those in power and empowered, those that are models for socially rewarded or recognized, traditional roles. When cultures look skyward and place a strong man with will and power at the summit, then Wotan or his equivalent is the ruling archetype, and power can become addictive.

THE UNDERWORLD

Nibelhome is the underground home of the Nibelungs, that is, an underworld realm. They are dwarves or gnomes who live underground and work as miners, smelters, or craftsmen at their smithies.

SYMBOLOGY OF SCENES

Like the underwater realm, the underworld usually symbol-izes the unconscious, and while there are similarities, the differences are significant. In contrast to the emotional depths that water usually represents, the underworld contains memo-ries, thoughts, and aspects of ourselves that we have put away. Everything too painful or too shameful or too unattractive or unacceptable to others to allow to show are the contents of this part of the personal unconscious, as well as anything about which we do not want to think and so repress or suppress, is kept down there.

Here too are gold and other treasures, the as-yet riches that have not been found and brought up into consciousness. Reflecting this awareness, the Roman name for the god of the underworld was Pluto, which meant "riches underground." Like the gold talents of the Bible, which were not to be buried and hoarded but to be used and increased, underworld gold is a metaphor for natural talents that need to be unearthed or buried abilities that need to be found and then refined and pro-cessed until we make something of them.

Hades was the name of the underworld as well as of the god whose realm it was in Greek mythology. The shades dwelt in Hades, images of those who had once lived and now were devoid of life. To exist in the underworld is also a metaphor for chronic depression, in which life seems gray, devoid of colora-tion and vitality. When we are depressed, we usually feel unat-tractive, even ugly, unfit to be in the company of successful others; we feel like a Nibelung, small, misshapen, oppressed.

The Greek god Hephaestus, who was the god of the forge, also had his smithy underground. He was a rejected cripple who worked with his hands, in contrast to the beautiful immortals of Mount Olympus. Hephaestus, too, could be called "a Nibelung"—as a designation for what is rejected in us, first by others and then by ourselves.

Whatever is discounted by the culture goes "underground" as well. In sky-god mythology, the mental realm and the divinities associated with the mind, will, abstract thought, and power exerted at a distance are honored. They live on the summit, while those who represent devalued attributes do not.

THE LAND

When humans are the main characters in any scene, the location is on land, where houses are built and trees grow. Instead of being under the surface of the river, we are on the riverbank. When Wotan becomes the Wanderer, he comes down to earth as well. The earth is the realm of everyday experience and ordinary consciousness.

THE RIVER

The Rhine is a metaphor for the river of life and the river of time. It flows by as historical time and yet is part of an eternal cycle.

SELECTED READINGS

I. THE OPERA

The *Ring* cycle first came alive for me when I became engrossed in the story and dialogue through reading the libretto of the opera. The translated version that I happened upon in the C. G. Jung Institute of San Francisco's library was Stewart Robb's. The Opera Guide Series on each of the four operas provided me with interpretive notes, history, thematic guides to the music leitmotifs, and Andrew Porter's translation of the libretto, which was my primary reference.

Wagner, Richard. *The Rhinegold/Das Rheingold*. English translation by Andrew Porter (1985). Opera Guide Series, no. 35. Edited by Nicholas John. Published in association with English National Opera and The Royal Opera. New York: Riverrun Press, 1985.

———. *The Ring of the Nibelung*. Translated, and with a foreword, by Stewart Robb. New York: Dutton, 1960.

———. *Siegfried*. English translation by Andrew Porter (1976). Opera Guide Series, no. 28. Edited by Nicholas John. Published in association with English National Opera and The Royal Opera. New York: Riverrun Press, 1984.

———. *Twilight of the Gods/Götterdämmerung*. English translation by Andrew Porter (1976). Opera Guide Series, no. 31. Edited by Nicholas John. Published in association with English National Opera and The Royal Opera. New York: Riverrun Press, 1985.

SELECTED READINGS

———. *The Valkyrie/Die Walküre*. English translation by Andrew Porter (1976). Opera Guide Series, no. 21. Edited by Nicholas John. Published in association with English National Opera and The Royal Opera. New York: Riverrun Press, 1983.

II. COMMENTARIES ON THE *RING* CYCLE

Robert Donington's *Wagner's Ring and Its Symbols: The Music and the Myth* (New York: St. Martin's Press, 1974; first published, 1963) is the classic, scholarly, Jungian interpretation of the *Ring* cycle. Donington's psychological perspective is as if the *Ring* cycle were Wotan's personal myth, with the other characters in the *Ring* cycle therefore aspects of Wotan's personality: for example, Brunnhilde and Fricka are aspects of Wotan's anima. Since myths are like collective dreams, and dreams can be interpreted from many valid perspectives, there is no one correct interpretation. Instead, there are many possible meanings. Other than Donington's book (which has an extensive bibliography), I did not read any other psychological interpretations of the *Ring* cycle.

III. PSYCHOLOGICAL PERSPECTIVE

Ring of Power is a clinically based, psychological perspective that grows out of my training and practice as a psychiatrist and Jungian analyst. It was influenced by my residency training in psychiatry that was psychoanalytically oriented, followed by training as a Jungian analyst. The *Collected Works of C. G. Jung* remains the major reference for Jungian thought on myths, symbols, structure of the psyche, psychological types, dream interpretation, and the archetypes of the collective unconscious, which provides a depth understanding of the individual psyche. The women's movement and its literature defined patriarchy and its effects upon individuals for me, after which I could see how people are influenced by archetypes within themselves and the expectations of family and society, as I described in *Goddesses in Everywoman* and *Gods in Everyman*. Alice Miller's books on narcissism and the effect abuse has on children contributed greatly to my clinical perspective, as has the literature on addictions, codependency, the dysfunctional family, and society.

Bolen, Jean Shinoda. *Gods in Everyman*. San Francisco: Harper & Row, 1989.

———. *Goddesses in Everywoman*. San Francisco: Harper & Row, 1984.

Bradshaw, John. *The Family*. Deerfield Beach, FL: Health Communications, 1988.

Jung, C. G. *Collected Works of C. G. Jung*. Edited by Herbert Read, Michael Fordham, and Gerald Adler; translated by R. F. C. Hull and William McGuire. Bollingen Series, no. 20. Princeton, NJ: Princeton Univ. Press, each volume individually dated.

Love, Patricia, with Jo Robinson. *The Emotional Incest Syndrome*. New York: Bantam, 1990.

Miller, Alice. *Drama of the Gifted Child and the Search for the True Self*. (Originally published as *Prisoners of Childhood*.) Translated by Ruth Ward. New York: Basic Books, 1981.

———. *For Your Own Good: Hidden Cruelty in Childrearing and the Roots of Violence*. Translated by Hildegarde and Hunter Hannu. New York: Farrar Straus Giroux, 1983.

Schaef, Anne Wilson. *When Society Becomes an Addict*. San Francisco: Harper & Row, 1987.

Steinem, Gloria. *Revolution From Within*. Boston: Little Brown, 1992.

Terr, Lenore. *Too Scared to Cry*. New York: Harper & Row, 1990.

SELECTED READINGS

IV. EMPOWERING THE FEMININE

If depreciation of feminine values, of the anima in men, and disempowerment of women are related to the disappearance of the goddess or the absence of a feminine aspect of divinity, this dishonored or missing feminine wisdom will need to return into the psyches of men and women and into the culture. These are books that provide insights into what was repressed and what can reappear and balance masculine qualities and values.

Eisler, Riane. *The Chalice and the Blade.* San Francisco: Harper & Row, 1987.

Gimbutas, Marija. *The Goddesses and Gods of Old Europe 6500–3500 B.C.: Myths and Cult Images.* rev. ed. Berkeley: University of California Press, 1982.

Pagels, Elaine. *The Gnostic Gospels.* New York: Vintage Books, 1981.

Spretnak, Charlene, ed. *The Politics of Women's Spirituality.* New York: Doubleday, 1982.

Stone, Merlin. *When God was a Woman.* New York: Harcourt Brace Jovanovich, 1976.

DISCOGRAPHY

THE COMPLETE RECORDINGS OF WAGNER'S
RING OF THE NIBELUNG

This is a list provided by Patrick J. Smith, editor of *Opera News*, of generally available commercial audio recordings.

Codes: (A) Brunnhilde, (B) Sieglinde, (C) Gutrune, (D) Fricka, (E) Siegmund, (F) Siegfried, (G) Mime, (H) Gunther, (I) Wotan, (J) Alberich, (K) Hagen, (L) Hunding

1958–66: London/Decca; (A) Nilsson, (B) Crespin, (C) Watson, (D) Flagstad, Ludwig, (E) King, (F) Windgassen, (G) Kuen, Stolze, (H) Fischer-Dieskau, (I) London, Hottor, (J) Neidlinger, (K) Frick, (L) Frick; Vienna Philharmonic Orchestra; Sir Georg Solti

1966–67: Phillips; (A) Nilsson, (B) Rysanek, (C) Dvořáková, (D) Burmeister, (E) King, (F) Windgassen, (G) Wohlfahrt, (H) Stewart, (I) Adam, (J) Neidlinger, (K) Greindl, (L) Nienstedt; Bayreuth Festival Orchestra; Karl Böhm

1966–70: Deutsche Grammophon; (A) Crespin, Dernesch, (B) Janowitz, (C) Janowitz, (D) Veasey, (E) Vickers, (F) Thomas, Brilioth, (G) Wohlfahrt, Stolze, (H) Stewart, (I) Fischer-Dieskau, Stewart, (J) Keleman, (K) Ridderbusch, (L) Talvela; Berlin Philharmonic Orchestra; Herbert von Karajan

1980–83: Eurodisc; (A) Altmeyer, (B) Norman, (C) Dvořáková, (D) Minton, (E) Jerusalem, (F) Kollo, (G) Schreier, (H) Nöcker,

(I) Adam, (J) Nimsgern, (K) Salminen, (L) Moll; Dresden Statt-skapelle; Marek Janowski

1988–92: Deutsche Grammophon: (A) Behrens, (B) Norman, (D) Ludwig, (E) Lakes, (F) Goldberg, (H) Weikl, (I) Morris, (J) Wlaschiha, (K) Salminen; Metropolitan Opera Orchestra: James Levine

THE COMPLETE VIDEO RECORDINGS OF WAGNER'S
DER RING DES NIELUNGEN

The Metropolitan Opera Production, first broadcast in 1990, and available individually or as a complete set on VHS or Laser Video Disc.

Das Rheingold: Morris, Ludwig, Jerusalem, Wlaschiha, Zed-nik, Rootering, Salminen; James Levine.

Die Walküre: Behrens, Norman, Ludwig, Lakes, Morris, Moll; James Levine.

Siegfried: Jerusalem, Morris, Zednik, Behrens, Wlaschiha, Svenden, Upshaw, Salminen; James Levine.

Götterdämmerung: Behrens, Jerusalem, Salminen, Ludwig, Raffell, Lisowska, Wlaschiha; James Levine.

INDEX

abandonment, 56–57, 184, 193, 203–205
abuse, 9, 24, 27, 90, 104, 162, 166, 169, 199, 203–204
abused child, 8, 24–25, 40, 72, 104, 109–110, 128, 156–157, 166, 196–197, 203
abusive cycle, 24, 25, 204, 205
abusive families, 104, 109, 131, 163
addictions, 12, 23, 27, 33, 62–64, 86, 115, 118–119, 126, 184, 196, 206, 228
"adult children," 107–109, 163, 167, 170–171, 173, 204
Agamemnon, 29–30
agreements, 28, 33, 65. See also law, treaties
Alberich the Nibelung, 4, 6, 10, 17–18, 20–22, 24–29, 33, 36, 40, 50, 94, 96, 134, 137, 140–141, 152, 156, 168
  as "adult child," 150–151
  as aspect of Wotan, 33, 37
  as Mime's opposite, 27–28
Alberich's curse, 116, 136, 146
alchemy, 178, 179
alcoholism, 33, 164, 200. See also dysfunctional family
Alexander the Great, 10
ambition, 7, 8, 32–33, 41, 81, 151, 204
anima, 32, 35–36, 127, 161, 169, 213–214
animus, 105, 118

apples, golden, 19, 34, 139. See also Freya
archetypes, 3, 10, 118, 123, 171, 216
  of authoritarian father, 24, 114, 210–212
  of father's daughter, 67–68, 83
  of hero, 170, 171
  of king, 78, 122
  of the Self, 37
  of traveler, 31
armor, 68, 101, 102, 128
ash tree, 45–47, 135, 139, 207, 216
Athena, 2, 67, 68
authoritarian
  father, 5, 59, 60, 67, 77, 208, 210–212, 218
  personality, 6–7, 80, 125, 214

bear, 90, 105, 106–109, 146
betrayal, 50, 51, 57, 128, 139, 142, 149, 161, 164–165, 167, 177
birdsong, 95, 147, 169
boar, 145, 148, 172
Brahma Kumari Sisters, 209
Brunnhilde, 2, 5, 8–11, 42, 44, 47–49, 50, 52, 88, 117, 132, 134–145, 161, 179, 185
  as abused victim, 128, 162–163, 167, 204
  as "adult child," 150–151
  as anima, 84, 213

as bride, 70, 97, 130–131,
  136–138, 147–148, 166, 185
as daughter, 66, 67
as developing, 68, 78, 175–176
asleep and awake, 59, 88, 99,
  102, 128–129
as slave, 51
as trophy, 102, 153
as wife, 146, 149
as wise, 98, 127
betrayed, 140, 144
burning, 46, 73
compassionate, 75–76, 79, 174
disobeys Wotan, 53, 55, 59, 129
punished, 56–59

Campbell, Joseph, 183, 190
charismatic leaders, 14, 37
children, 4, 27, 60, 65. See also
  abused child, dysfunctional
  family
choice, 13, 82, 84–85, 182, 194,
  195, 206
Christianity, 12, 209, 216
codependency, 7, 33, 60, 66–67,
  79, 126, 131, 184, 205–206
collective unconscious, 36, 122,
  208, 215
compassion, 9, 35, 42, 60, 84,
  110, 203, 205, 220
compulsions, 119, 180, 205. See
  also obsessions
confusion, 165–166
conjugal rights, 72, 141
consciousness, 13, 123, 182, 227
contracts, 28, 50, 126. See also
  agreements, law
control, 10, 30, 84, 108, 118, 197,
  211. See also power,
  authoritarian father
courage, 60, 126–127, 175, 190,
  220

darkness, 18, 22, 47

daughter, 9, 65, 72, 77–78. See
  also Brunnhilde, father's
  daughter
death, 21, 124, 193
demonic leaders, 14, 37
denial, 31, 33, 123, 196
dependency, 108, 185. See also
  addictions, codependency
depression, 6–8, 12, 62, 103, 162,
  205–206
disobedience, Brunnhilde's, 55,
  66, 77, 83
divinity, 37, 80, 186
divorce, 184, 188
domination, 11, 26, 56, 57, 60,
  163, 208
Donner, 16
dragon, 119
  blood, 95, 119, 120, 158
  killing, 86, 96, 115, 118, 137,
    147, 161
The Drama of the Gifted Child,
  111
dream interpretation, 2–3, 13,
  74, 106, 122–123, 135, 166,
  169, 181, 194. See also
  mythology
drugs, 33, 46. See also alcoholism
dwarf figure, 4, 16, 26, 89, 117.
  See also Alberich, Mime
dysfunctional
  marriages, 5, 60, 61, 105, 203
  relationships, 7, 132
dysfunctional family, 4, 26, 59,
  60, 66, 76, 112, 120, 126,
  151, 156, 162–163, 179
  adult children of, 154, 161
  and abused daughters, 128
  breaking cycle of, 2, 9, 183
  diagnosis of, 120
  patterns of, 109, 114, 166,
    198
  rules of, 172, 197
  secrets of, 121, 152, 174, 186

INDEX

Easter, 193, 194

Eisler, Riane, 215

emotional
abandonment, 60, 157
complex, 118, 120. *See also*
feelings
inability, 28, 32, 77, 83, 164,
200
incest, 104

empathy, 66, 110, 112, 162

enantiodromia, 214–215, 218

envy, 22, 111, 157

Epidauros, 13

epiphany, 190

Erda, 16, 38, 44, 68, 98, 101, 123,
134, 136, 175, 213, 217
and mountains, 228
and present/future, 38, 50
as Brunnhilde's mother, 50, 80,
128
as wisdom, 82, 88, 122, 176

Erda's
daughters, 135. *See also* the
Norns
sleep, 99, 217
warning, 22, 50

Erikson, Erik, 214

Fafner, 16, 18–19, 20, 22–23, 34,
90, 93–95, 111
as dragon, 50, 54, 115–118

fame, 18, 23, 151, 176. *See also*
power

family dynamics, 112, 114,
120–121. *See also* dysfunctional family

Fasolt, 16, 18–20, 22–23, 34, 50,
116

father, 68, 72, 77, 127, 211. *See*
also authoritarian father,
Wotan

father god, 1, 210

Father Sky, 216

father's daughter, 67–68, 83, 125

fear, 102, 109–110, 117–118, 163
of death and aging, 98, 124
Siegfried's lack of, 94–95, 97,
117, 184

feeling personality type, 112

feelings, 61, 83, 110–111, 127
emerging, 7, 114, 198, 206
of impotence, 24
of safety, 11, 197–198
price of, 69–70
repression of, 61–62, 65–67,
76, 78–79, 110–111, 120, 152,
164, 196–197, 200, 206

feminine
aspect, 35–36, 84, 115, 219. *See*
also anima
values, 30, 42, 72
wisdom, 122, 214. *See also*
Erda

fire, 46, 73, 74, 101, 179
as purification, 178, 185
of destruction, 136
of feeling, 103, 186
of funeral, 149, 150, 178

fire god, 19, 59

fire ring, 58, 89, 139, 140

Flosshilde, 16

forced marriage, 72. *See also* rape

For Your Own Good, 40

freedom, 9, 11, 13, 21, 104,
112–114, 197, 206

free hero, 49–50, 58, 64–65, 83

Freya, 4, 16, 19, 20, 22, 28–32,
34, 38, 80, 116

Fricka, 2, 4, 7, 16, 18, 22–23,
31–33, 49, 53, 79–80
as goddess of marriage, 44, 48,
63
as voice of reality, 64

Froh, 16

funeral pyre, 149–150, 178. *See*
also fire

Gerhilde, 44

giants, 16, 19, 20, 22, 115, 164.
    See also Fafner, Fasolt
Gibich, 134, 152
Gibichung hall, 148, 162
Gibichungs, 134, 137, 138, 140,
    142, 150–151, 152, 153, 161,
    170
  as "adult children," 150, 151
  as opportunists, 182
Gimbutas, Marija, 215
The Gnostic Gospels, 217
the goddess, 215, 216
god of underworld, 229
gods' destruction, 32, 50, 99, 103,
    124, 178, 182, 185, 193–194
gold, 23, 27, 116, 146, 155
  as symbol, 14, 177, 229
gold hoard, 20–22, 34, 50, 94
Götterdämmerung, 5
Grane, 54, 102, 137, 150, 177
grief, 63, 175. See also suffering
Grimgerde, 44
Grimhild, 134, 137
guilt and sex, 72, 74, 103, 108,
    111
Gunther, 137–139, 140, 141–148,
    152–155, 158, 161, 165, 168,
    170, 182
Gutrune, 134, 137–139, 141–144,
    146–149, 152–154, 158, 159,
    165, 172, 174–175

Hades, 30, 229
Hagen, 40, 134, 137, 139,
    140–141, 145, 147–150, 173,
    175
  as adult child, 203
  as hate, 141, 155, 200
  as murderer, 167, 168, 172
  character of, 154, 169
healing, 12, 13, 220
heathen (heiden), 216
Helmwige, 44
Hephaestus, 229

Hera, 4, 48, 62, 63
Hermes, 19, 30
hero, 9, 50, 75, 114, 116, 118,
    152, 161, 171–172, 185, 200
  archetype, 172, 183–184, 185
  as father and son, 124
  fatherless, 114
  free, 49–50, 58, 64–65, 83. See
    also Siegfried, Siegmund
  sociopathic, 112
Hero with a Thousand Faces,
    183
Hill, Anita, 168
Hitler, 10, 37, 39, 40
horses, magic, 44, 101, 129, 150,
    185
humiliation, 1, 4, 24–26, 40–41,
    56, 63, 154–156
Hunding, 8, 44–48, 50–53, 61,
    63–64, 70, 74, 89
husband's role, 32, 56, 60, 78,
    147
Hussein, Saddam, 39, 40

identification, negative, 24, 113
identity, 110, 112, 114
immortality, 16, 32, 75, 123, 131
incestuous relationship, 5, 8, 60,
    70, 76–78
individuation, 84, 184
Indo-European tribes, 215
Industrial Revolution, 27
inflation of ego, 122
inhibitions, 170, 197
initiatory experience, 130
inner story, 52, 84–85, 114–115,
    125, 184
innocence, 29, 30, 72
integrity, 12, 127, 192
intellect, 110, 111, 154
intuition, 114, 120, 158, 169, 174
invisibility, 20, 21. See also
    Tarnhelm
isolation, 34, 164

Jehovah, 228
Jesus Christ, 193, 209
Johnson, Sonia, 194
Jones, Reverend James, 37
Jonestown, 37
Jung, C. G., 36–37, 105, 214–215
justice, 127, 197, 204

Kennedy,
    John, 40
    Joseph Jr., 40
    Joseph P., 39, 40
    Robert, 40
King Lear, 122
King, Martin Luther, Jr., 191

law, 28, 60–61, 71, 112, 135, 150,
    187–190, 217
light, 17, 18, 47, 71, 72, 103, 123
"Light Alberich," 33, 92
location in *The Rhinegold*,
    227–230
Loge, 16, 19–22, 30–31, 33, 37,
    50, 59, 64, 136, 150, 177
love, 2, 4, 10–11, 20, 24, 29, 35,
    41–42, 50, 57, 59, 61–62, 68,
    70–71, 77, 79, 82–84, 97,
    197
    above law, 127
    and empathy, 110
    and sex, 102
    and soul, 137
    as Brunnhilde's legacy, 150
    as gold, 177
    for power, 156
    of mother, 114
    renouncing, 202
lying, 120, 121, 144, 152, 158,
    162, 167
Luther, Martin, 191

manipulativeness, 104, 120. *See
    also* Mime
marital rape, 142, 164

marriage, 7, 70, 105, 152–153,
    155, 188, 214
    as institution, 32, 46, 56, 62
    as sacred, 36, 63
martyr parent, 5, 103–104, 106
masculine traits, 105, 118, 122
mask, as persona, 151
master of woman, 127, 131, 137
memory, 73–74, 147, 198–199
men, 8, 33, 201, 212
    expectations of, 111, 112
    nonpatriarchal, 9
mentors, 113, 124–125
Mercury, 30
mermaids, 34
messenger god, 19, 30
Metis, 68, 217
midlife crisis, 195, 214, 218
Miller, Alice, 40, 111
Mime, 5, 16, 20, 26–28, 88–90,
    92–96, 103–108, 111,
    113–114, 116–117, 119,
    121-122, 158, 162, 199
    as abused child, 110
    self-pitying, 91
mortality, 5, 56, 123. *See also*
    Brunnhilde, gods'
    destruction
mother
    as martyr, 104
    devouring, 105–106
    figure, 35, 74, 79–80, 102, 129,
        152, 155
    realm, 123, 219
mountains as symbol, 227
Mount Olympus, 228, 229
Mount Sinai, 228
"Mr. Wolf," 39
multiple personalities, 197
music, 149, 150. *See also*
    birdsong
mythology, 1, 2, 3, 16, 19, 80, 84,
    92, 114, 209, 217, 229
    males in, 30

Nag Hammadi scrolls, 217
narcissism, 1, 7, 60, 65, 67, 77,
    80, 124–125, 156, 182, 204
Native American, 216
nature, 11, 121–123
need, 10, 46–47. *See also* Notung
Nibelhome, 16, 228
Nibelung (dwarf), 4, 16, 24,
    25–28, 134, 145, 152
Nibelung hoard, 96, 116, 138.
    See also *Ring of the
    Nibelung*
Nibelung type, 20, 30, 113, 229
the Norns, 98, 108, 134–136,
    215–217
Notung, 47, 55, 76, 89, 90,
    92–93, 95, 140, 144, 147

obedience, 1, 33, 68, 76, 79, 84,
    162–163, 165
obsessions, 23, 25–27, 33, 36, 38,
    64, 84, 116, 119. *See also*
    addictions
Odin, 16
opportunist, 158–159, 161. *See
    also* Gibichungs
Ortlinde, 44
outcast, 9, 25, 56, 65, 69, 71. *See
    also* Siegmund, Brunnhilde

pagan, pagani, 216
Pagel, Elaine, 217
paranoia, 20, 116, 117
parenting, 11, 91, 107–109,
    112–113, 126, 157
Parks, Rosa, 191
passivity, 7, 60, 162–163, 165
"pathognomonic," 120
patriarchy, 6, 9, 11, 29, 33, 41, 60,
    69, 72, 80, 84, 104, 122, 130,
    151, 176, 181, 210, 212, 215
    end of, 206, 218
    in inner life, 219
paying the price, 18, 19, 31, 34

Persephone, 30
persona, 151–153
Pluto, 229
power, 2, 8–9, *14*, 18, 23, 34, 37,
    41–*42*, 62, 81–82, 84,
    120–121, 124, 167, 174, 197,
    201–202, 205, 212
    addiction, 27, 33
    as substitute for love, 1, 10–11,
    48, 61–62, 82, 167
    issues, 172
    seduction of, 28, 41, 64, 181
    to control others, 77, 202, 208
psychological
    complex, 115
    growth, 38, 119, 130
    interpretations, 3
    principles, 11
    questions, 92
    typology, 112
psychopaths, 200
psychosomatic illness, 7
psychotherapy, 107, 113, 127,
    169, 184, 196
punishment, 6, 58, 63, 79, 98,
    104, 126–127, 157, 197
purification, *132*, 145, 178

rage, 66, 77–79, 83, 100, 118,
    128, 163
Rainbow Bridge, 16, 23
Raj Yoga, 209
rape, 1, 73, 74, 142, 164, 199
rationalization, 30–31
ravens, 148, 149
recovery program, 9, 12, 167, 179
redemption, 150
Reformation, 191–192
rejection, 24, 25, 26, 69
relationship, 61, 111, 117, 123,
    129. *See also* love
remorse, 81, 111
repression, 78, 124, 165, 171,
    198. *See also* feelings

resentment, 28, 103
resurrection, 192–193
revenge, 18, 24, 26, 28, 41, 63,
    75, 145, 167. *See also*
    vengeance
Revolution from Within, 25
Rhine, 6, 17, 25, 138–141, 146,
    150, 177, 179–180, 185, 230
The Rhinegold (Das Rheingold),
    4, 15–17, 23, 64, 73, 82, 212
Rhinegold, 6, *14*, 16–17, 36–37,
    134, 146, 180
Rhinemaidens, *14*, 16–18, 20, 23,
    134, 140, 146, 149, 150, 179,
    207, 227
    as symbols, 34–36
ridicule, 24–25, 155, 157
Ring cycle, 39, 184, 195, 203,
    207, 219, 227
ring of fire, 58–59, 89, 97, 100,
    139–140
ring of power, 4, 16, 18, 20, 23–24,
    26, 40, 49, 50, 64–65, 82,
    93–94, 96–97, 99, 117–118,
    120, 138, 140–141, 146, 148,
    156, 172–173, 184, 207, 219
    and lies, 199–200
    curse on, 21–22, 24, 38, 116,
        140, 146–147, 149
    purified, 150, 178, 180, 185
Ring of the Nibelung, 2, 3,
    10–11, 39, 41, 79, 82, 84,
    181–183, 202–203, 212, 217,
    219, 228
ring of the Nibelung, 4, 6, 23,
    49, 80, 88, 92, *132*, 137
Rossweise, 44

sacrifice of women, 1, 23, 150,
    190, 192
sanctuary, 11, 12, 13, 73, 197,
    198
"Saturday" phase, 193, 194
scapegoat, 24, 104, 186

Schwertleite, 44
security, 10, 23, 29, 30
the Self, 36–37, 84, 179, 180,
    185, 216, 220
self-esteem, 7–8, 11–12, 25–26,
    105
self-knowledge, 3, 117
self-pity, 49, 65
sensitivity, 14, 69, 78
separateness, 60, 114
sex, 23, 36, 62, 72, 75, 102–103,
    130, 153–155, 164
sexual
    abuse, 74, 87, 128, 163
    exposure, 56, 57, 127
    power, 34, 36, 199
the shadow, 38, 179, 185, 220
shame, 72, 76, 154
shapechanging, 138
Siegfried, 5, 33, 212
Siegfried, 8, 53–55, 88, 96,
    97–99, 101, 103, 113–114,
    119, 122, 134, 153, 168,
    174–175
    and Brunnhilde, 110, 129,
        137–141, 143, 146–147, 161,
        165, 167, 185
    as adult child, 89–92, 108–110,
        121, 150–151
    as opportunist, 158–159
    as son successor, 122, 124–125
    as unsocialized, 100, 111, 117,
        154, 162, 166, 169
    frees himself, 93, 120
    kills dragon, *86*, 115–116
Siegfried's
    awakening, 102, 128
    death, 145, 155, 172
    funeral pyre, *132*, 149–150,
        177, 180
Sieglinde, 5, 7, 44–47, 51–52,
    117, 134
    as victim, 72–74
    meaning of, 70–71, 76, 83

Sieglinde's
  death, 80, 89
  escape, 53, 55, 127, 129
  son, 54, 88, 102. *See also*
    Siegfried
Siegmund, 5, 8, 9–11, 39, 44,
    46–48, 51–53, 89, 127
  as compassionate hero, 68–70,
    71, 75, 79, 83
  as "free hero," 50, 64–65, 80
  sword, 55, 76. *See also* Notung
Siegrune, 44
sky god, 229–230
slaves, 27, 37, 50, 131
sleep, 56, 58, 84, 98, 99, 100,
    123, 126, 129, 164
sociopath, 111, 112
sons as power, 40, 50, 65, 105
Sophia, 217
soul, 84, 121, 127, 161, 179, 184.
    See also anima
spear, 59, 89, 94, 101, 135, 139,
    144–145, 167, 217
  as law, 28, 126
spiral pattern, 10
spring, 135, 216, 217
status, 23, 33, 159
Steinem, Gloria, 25
Stone, Merlin, 215
suffering, 167, 175, 176, 184,
    190, 193, 203
suicide, 169, 178, 192
sunlight, 71, 101, 102, 146
surrogate families, 113
survivors of dysfunctional
    families, 113
sword, 46–47, 49, 52, 76, 89, 90,
    92, 99, 101, 107, 110. *See
    also* Notung
  forging one's own, 108, 114,
    118–120

Tao, 216
Tarnhelm, 16, 20–22, 27, 88,

  96–97, 117, 138–141, 144,
    161
temenos, 11, 12, 13
Ten Commandments, 228
terrorists, 156–157
therapeutic relationship, 73
thinking clearly, 67, 117–118
thinking personality type, 112
time, 74, 122, 123
transformation, 10, 12–13, 179,
    181, 189, 192–194
transition, 119, 209, 218
trauma, 73, 79, 198
treachery, 143–144, 147, 172
treaties, 81, 135. *See also* law
tricksters, 21, 30, 31. *See also*
    Loge, Hermes
Troy, 30
truth, 60, 119, 122, 127, 149, 152,
    167, 178, 181, 183–184, 187,
    196
  acts of, 192–197
  as fire, *132*, 179, 186
  moments of, 184–195, 196
  speaking, 7, 31, 172
turning points, 186–195
twelve-step groups, 9, 12, 179
The Twilight of the Gods, 5, 39,
    151, 192, 207, 213, 215, 219
tyrants, 11, 26, 200, 211

uncertainty, 186, 192, 193–194, 195
unconditional love, 5, 13, 108
the unconscious, 122, 164, 227, 229
unconsciousness, 58, 78. *See
    also* sleep
underworld, 26, 216, 227

Valhalla, 4, 9, 16, 18, 20, 22, 23,
    29, 30, 32, 34, 39, 44, 48, 50,
    52, 57, 75, 103, 116, 123,
    131, 139, 140, 151
  igniting, *132*, 136, 149–150,
    177, 185, 207, 219

the Valkyrie, 5, 44, 47, 88, 131,
134, 165, 174, 185. *See also*
Brunnhilde
Valkyries, 44, 54, 56, 80, 139,
176, 228
The Valkyrie, 4, 9, 59, 60, 64, 83,
84, 117, 212
vengeance, 101, 148, 155–157,
177, 202. *See also* revenge
victimization, 5, 72, 74, 104,
128, 169, 185. *See also* abuse
violence, 12, 167, 169
virgin goddess, 83, 131
virginity, 44, 68, 78, 102, 127,
130–131
vulnerability, 9, 72, 131, 164

Wagner, Richard, 39, 149
Die Walküre, 4. See also *The
Valkyrie*
Walse, 46–48, 81
the Walsungs, 44, 48, 58
Waltraute, 44, 134, 139, 140
the Wanderer, 6, 81, 88, 92, 118,
122, 124, 139, 213, 230. *See
also* Wotan
warriors, 44, 67–68, 131, 215
water, 75, 179–180, 216–217
wealth, 23, 27, 176. *See also*
gold, power
wedding, 46–47, 142, 144, 153
Wellgunde, 16
Western civilizations, 215, 218,
228
wife, 32, 60, 71, 77, 152, 155
will, 6, 57, 105, 127, 155
wisdom, 82, 96, 98, 122, 135,
149–150, 169, 175–177, 217,
220. *See also* Erda
Wittenburg, 192

"Woeful," 45, 46. *See also*
Siegmund
Woglinde, 16
Wolf, 39, 46, 68
Wolfcub, 39, 46, 68, 70
women, 1, 12, 104–105, 111, 128,
167–168, 201
as property, 73, 142, 153, 155
women's movement, 9
woodbird, 88, 95–97, 99,
119–121, 147
Wotan, 2, 5–7, 10–11, 16, 18, 20,
22–23, 28, 29, 30, 32, 33–34,
37, 39, 42, 44, 48, 50, 81,
134–136, 145. *See also*
Walse, Wanderer, Wolf.
and death, 123, 124, 139, 150,
185, 207, 218
and mountains, 228
as abusive father, 59, 66, 89, 131
as archetype, 28, 80, 82, 84,
176
as Light-Alberich, 33
building Valhalla, 151
Wotan father, 79
Wotan's
character, 48–49, 50, 64, 76,
78, 81, 121, 127, 212
daughters, 7–8
marriage, 6, 7, 48–49, 62
ravens, 147
sons, 8
spear, 19, 126, 135, 217
will, 84, 101, 117, 204
wrath, 51, 54, 57, 118, 127, 165
Wright, Deborah, 193

youth, 25, 29, 116

Zeus, 2, 4, 16, 30, 62–63, 228